PENGUIN BOOKS

WAIS NA MISIS: THE WISE HOMEMAKER

Neri Miranda has been dubbed as 'Wais Na Misis' because of her impressive entrepreneurial feats while juggling being a full-time mom and a homemaker—as evidenced by her equally educational and entertaining social media posts. She holds a bachelor's degree in business administration from the University of Baguio, Philippines, and is currently finishing her master's in business administration at the same university.

This awe-inspiring mom of three doesn't let a minute go to waste. She either spends it learning or earning. If not in front of her laptop researching, you can find her all over the country, personally managing multiple businesses.

Neri has amassed 3.6 million followers. Before becoming a successful entrepreneur, she gained nationwide popularity as the sixth runner-up of a local star-search television show and has starred in many television shows and movies.

WAIS NA MISIS
The Wise Homemaker

Neri Miranda

PENGUIN BOOKS

An imprint of Penguin Random House

PENGUIN BOOKS

USA | Canada | UK | Ireland | Australia
New Zealand | India | South Africa | China | Southeast Asia

Penguin Books is part of the Penguin Random House group of companies
whose addresses can be found at global.penguinrandomhouse.com

Published by Penguin Random House SEA Pte. Ltd
9, Changi South Street 3, Level 08-01,
Singapore 486361

First published in Penguin Books by Penguin Random House SEA 2023

ISBN 9789815162035

Typeset in Garamond by MAP Systems, Bengaluru, India

www.penguin.sg

Contents

Contents

Prologue

My life is nothing special. Whatever hardships I have experienced while growing up, certainly someone else on this planet may have experienced as well, or even worse. Then what makes my life story worth reading?

Nothing, except the fruits of my teamwork with God, the recipient of letters I wrote during my childhood.

As a child growing up in a dysfunctional household and experiencing an unconventional childhood (you'll learn more about this in the next pages of the book; so, keep on reading!) I had no one to share my aches and pains with. I had a few select friends then, yes, but I didn't have a confidant whom I could rant to or process my feelings with.

My parents had to deal with their own issues so, what would a kid like me do then?

I turned to God.

Although I knew I couldn't see or hear Him, I knew deep in my heart that He was there. When the people I could see and touch, couldn't and sometimes wouldn't give me solutions, I wrote letters to God, in my diary, in the hopes that my questions, rants, and concerns would be addressed. Every bit of joy and pain, mostly the latter, I wrote about in my letter to Him every day.

I remember, on days when I couldn't understand why my mom acted the way she did or why some kids would deliberately exclude me from their activities because they either found me weird or maybe I was too poor for their taste, I would grab my diary and start writing letters to God. I'd usually consume at least five pages of my notebook just sharing my frustrations and asking God hundreds of questions. When I couldn't find the right words to say, I'd sometimes doodle my emotions out. I was a child. I knew nothing of the kind of world I was shoved into. All I had were questions like 'Why me, Lord?' or 'Am I a bad person? Why am I experiencing all these misfortunes?' but no definite answers.

These types of questions would still pop up in my head once in a while but now I know better. I am older and, thankfully, wiser. Looking back, I realized that God had been training me all along. This realization reminded me of what the late Steve Jobs once said: 'You can't connect the dots looking forward; you can only connect them looking backward. So you have to trust that the dots will somehow connect in your future. You have to trust in something—your gut, destiny, life, karma, whatever. This approach has never let me down, and it has made all the difference in my life.'

I trusted God.

As I was writing this book, trying to recall all the past events that have led me to this day, I saw how God never left my side and His love for me never changed. He has been my training coach all these years, standing with me on my mountain tops and sitting beside me in my valleys where I thought I had no one.

Remembering the entries from my old diary, I now appreciate how God allowed hardships to happen so I could become a better person; learn from the people who have hurt and disappointed me so I wouldn't do the same to others; and not take for granted all the blessings that I now have, that at some point I only used to pray for. The diary pages also reminded me that, as a child, God had already planned my days and the assignments I needed to accomplish so that my future-self and the next generations would benefit from it.

I mean, how would I know, right? I seriously had no clue at that time. But had I given up, had I joined the dark side and evolved into a rebellious and vengeful person, I'd never have gotten the chance to live the life God had planned for me.

This is one of the reasons why I keep saying to everyone who asks me for life advice: '*Kapit lang!*' (Keep holding on!). I don't mean to sound insensitive because I understand that we all come from different backgrounds, with different levels of privileges. But what I mean to say when I say Kapit lang is that no matter how difficult it may seem, hold on to the hope that the God who holds your future will be with you until the end. He will never let go of your hand.

In this lifetime, we all have roles to play. We have our crosses to bear and we have purposes to fulfil. I believe that I went through what I'd gone through so there'd be one less person to walk this earth clueless and possibly hopeless.

Apart from being my coach, I also realized how great of a teammate God has always been. He supplied everything that I needed, even what I thought I wouldn't need, he provided for me, too.

When we didn't have enough money, he dropped business ideas for my mom and I to work on. When I wanted to attend a school camping activity but didn't have the money to push through with it, God gave me friends with the biggest hearts who helped me join the camp. When the world pushed me to be angry, He gave me the peace and self-control that I know only He could give. When I prayed for a better life, He not only gave me what I thought I needed. He gave me business ideas, business partners, mentors, friends, a husband, and a family to strive hard for and live life with.

Along with the blessings are the setbacks and challenges that He still allows me to experience, so I don't become complacent, and I can continuously learn from life. Without the bad, I wouldn't have appreciated that life has been good all along. If it weren't for the mix, there wouldn't even be a *Wais Na Misis* but just … you know, 'Misis' or 'Clueless na Misis' to be exact.

I've been taught so much in this lifetime that I would like to pay it forward through this book. May this serve as your handy-dandy survival guide as you journey into the intimidating world of motherhood and entrepreneurship. Each page is brimming with meaty tips and tricks that I have learned from the best mentor I've ever had—LIFE.

But, take note, this is not an instructional book that will tell you all the exact steps I took from steps 1 to 3 to get me from points A to B. I may have a few, but you get the idea!

Since we all lead different lives, I fully understand that a cookie-cutter solution is not the best way to address it.

All I have in this book are detailed stories from my past and present that I am gladly sharing with you. Some have never been told on social media or shared in interviews, while most are the stories that you may have probably read in one of my many posts.

On every page are anecdotes, filled with my learnings, that I'm giving you the permission to take apart, assemble and disassemble, mix and match according to what you are going through at the moment. You have the power to choose. Pick out the ones from my story that you think you can best use in a given situation. You can also tweak it and make it your own. Just don't forget to pass on the technique and keep the new and improved cycle running.

If you have enjoyed and learned from the snippets of my life as a Wais Na Misis through my Instagram and Facebook posts, you'll most certainly get a kick out of some of the untold stories you'll find in the pages of this book.

As I have mentioned many times, life wasn't always easy for me. It just appeared to be that way because when life threw me lemons I didn't dodge or flinch. Instead, I caught every one and turned the bunch into lemonade, lemon meringue pie, lemon-scented hand soap, and home deodorizer, and sold them all! I'd sometimes wonder when another lemon would come my way just so I can use it to my advantage again.

You get the picture.

So, my fellow Wais Na Misis, allow me to hold your hand, and together, let's leave this world in a better state than we've found it.

Take a deep breath, let's go!

PART 1: SAVE Your Energy, SPEND Your Day WAIS-ly!

Chapter 1

I Grew Up Poor but My Mindset Was Rich

Let me paint you a picture of my life before you knew me as Neri the actress, Chito Miranda's wife, and a budding entrepreneur with several businesses and investments, which you've most probably seen on my social media pages.

If there's any childhood anecdote that has helped keep me stay grounded, it is the fact that I was born on the ground. I wasn't born on a bed of roses, to borrow a line from one of Jon Bon Jovi's famous songs in the 90s (let me warn you that this isn't the only 90s reference in this book). Instead, I was born on a linoleum-laden soil, in an unusual birthplace called the *silong*.

The silong is the space between the floor of a traditional Filipino *bahay kubo* (country house) and the soil where it stands. Its main purpose was to protect the house from being reached by flood water or mud during the rainy season. Apart from that, it can also be used as a storage area and shelter for chickens, pigs, and other farm animals you can think of. The height's approximately a metre or a bit more, and one would have to crouch to be able to enter it. I would like to refer to it as a basement that's not exactly the basement you'd typically see in Western movies—where it doubles as a toolshed or a garage, and looks fairly livable. As much as I am tempted to call it that, ours was nothing like it.

The one I was born in was a makeshift, basement-like area in my grandmother's old colonial bahay kubo in the locality of Matain, Subic, Zambales. It was our home. A home for all six of us in the family (I am the youngest of four children) until I was about three or four years old.

After that, we would move from one house to another depending on the situation we were in. Sometimes it was because my parents simply wanted to try and live in another city and other times, it was because we couldn't pay our rent in full.

If my memory serves me right, we had moved around twenty times during my younger days. Since it was my reality then and I'd considered it normal, I lived each day with contentment, not looking for something better. After all, I had no other experience to compare it to. In my mind, it was just how life was until my dad, who had worked as a local firefighter in our town in Subic, got a job as a firefighter instructor in Saudi Arabia when I was two years old.

Based on my mom's stories, we were able to move into a house that was slightly bigger than the usual ones we would live in; and we had surprisingly lasted longer there than our stays in our previous houses combined. It wasn't the best, because we had to do some repair work, but it was spacious and had more rooms. With the home upgrade came better meals, too. We'd have at least three full meals per day plus some snacks in between. But each full meal was no fancier than a steaming cup of rice and a small bowl of whatever available ingredients were in the kitchen to fry or blanch.

Oh, and we still couldn't eat at a nearby fast-food joint or treat ourselves to a gourmet meal on a whim. My siblings and I were only able to enjoy the oiliness of crispy french fries or the glorious cheese pull of a pizza whenever there would be a momentous occasion worth celebrating, like my brother's graduation.

My mom, a housewife and the original smarty pants when it comes to doing business and freelancing, would sometimes bring home a box of Dunkin' Donuts and a plastic container filled with warm food. This was after spending a day selling Tupperware products and other sorts of knick-knacks. On days when we'd crave something delicious and didn't have enough cash because my dad's remittance was delayed, my mom would send me to the nearby *sari-sari* store (small neighbourhood variety store) to buy canned sardines for lunch and a bottle of ice-cold cola, all on credit.

I could say we weren't dirt-poor but because my dad had mishandled his money, we weren't able to live a comfortable life as per society's standards. There would be times when we weren't able to pay our tuition fees or we were forced to skip school, all four of us, because we didn't have money to pay for our transportation. As soon as we were able to go back to class, we'd just casually tell our teachers that everyone in our family got sick thus our absence for a day or two. But the truth was, my dad just wasn't able to send his monthly provision on time. And because of this, it forced my mom—who was single-handedly raising us in the Philippines—to think of clever ways to make ends meet on her own.

Having seen how my mom strategized to make use of her day to bring something delicious to the table when my dad's provisions didn't arrive on time, I learned that starting small isn't something to be ashamed of. I saw that it didn't matter if she only had a few hundred pesos as capital for her business or a few tubs of hot rice meals to sell for the day. I saw from how she handled the challenge that for as long as you have the persistence and determination to earn and make an honest living with the resources at hand, you'll stay a few steps closer to your goal. Hard work will always beat talent anytime.

With this mindset, I have learned …

WAIS TIP #1: START SMALL, DREAM BIGGER!

When it comes to business, I have no issues with building things from scratch. Sure, it would be nice if everything was handed to me on a silver platter and I'll just have to wait for the harvest. Who doesn't want instant money?! But, you see, there's nothing more rewarding than to nurture an idea from infancy and witness it transform into the full-grown income generator I had hoped for and planned that it would be.

Since I grew up with nothing but my desire to live a better life, I have been so used to working my way through and up every single time. Because I knew that I would always need to diligently start from step 1, confidently, until I reached the final step.

As a child, having my little world and giving no care for anyone's business served me quite well, too. My mind was trained to just focus on my personal race. I didn't stop to look on either side and check if I was faster than the others or if they were already gaining on me.

This mindset came in handy when I had an idea of building a small backyard piggery brewing in my then-ten-year-old mind. I honestly didn't know where the idea came from. I must've seen one of my neighbours or I might have overheard it being mentioned during a random conversation between adults.

I just knew I needed to do something about this idea.

I didn't care if pursuing it would make me look silly in front of our neighbours. It also didn't bother me a bit if raising pigs for slaughter at that age would mean my classmates would and could make fun of me anytime. I simply wanted to make money and give whatever I was able to generate to my mom. That was and still is my goal: to work and earn, so my mom would be able to finally rest.

Soon enough, I found myself taking care of two piglets my mom had purchased with her own money. Taking care of the piglets meant me, the instigator of this crazy idea, having to stomach hours and hours of pig poop smell because, hey, I was brave enough to scoop it out and clean up after the cute, fat, and muddy moneymakers. I was in charge of the dirty work. It was literally dirty, to say the least, because I had to produce the slop, too. I would feed the piglets with my own teeny tiny hands until they had grown big enough to be butchered and sold.

As a petite ten-year-old, I would go around the neighbourhood in the late afternoon and be finished before dusk. I would carry an old bucket that was almost half my size then, knock on my neighbours' doors, and ask them to fill my container with their food scraps or *kaning baboy* as we'd like to call pig's food in Filipino.

Forgive me if you're reading this while having your dinner. But a mix of random leftovers, wet and dry, would be poured into my bucket by every neighbour who was more than happy to have meal scraps taken off their hands. Yucky, right? But I didn't mind. Weirdly enough I seemed to enjoy every bit of the collection process and I didn't feel like I was working at all!

I clearly remember I had fun while I was roaming around the neighbourhood trying to fill my bucket. On the rare occasions when I would get bored or discouraged (remember I was still a child!), I would occasionally take a peek into the half-filled bucket on the way to the next house and try to identify the type of vegetable or meat that was in it. Sometimes I would see cabbage leaves and cubed carrots sitting on top of the thick and yucky mixture. Rice was a staple; vegetable peelings, too.

As disgusting as it may sound, this little game of mine had kept me entertained for the duration of my 'job'. Because I knew that when I was able to fill the large four-feet plastic drum beside the pigpen, where the collected kaning baboy was permanently stored, my adorable yet demanding oinking moneymakers would have more than enough food to last for a day or two.

Because I had my eyes set on a goal for me and my family, it almost didn't bother me when I had to carry the full bucket, transfer its contents into the bigger drum, go back around the neighbourhood, and repeat the same process until it was filled. I religiously did it with a genuine smile on my sunburnt face and beads of sweat on my forehead while ignoring the possibility of tripping and eventually being covered with slop. What a sight it would've been!

Thank God, none of it happened. The only challenge that tested my desire to succeed in this little venture of mine was that I had to face the dreaded Subic highway. To reach more neighbouring houses, I had to cross the highway multiple times during the process of gathering slop until the huge 'mother drum' had been filled. Remembering those days, it must have been tiring for little Neri. Kids my age then were supposed to be either taking naps or playing in the streets but not raising pigs. But, as I said, I had big dreams for me and my mom—even bigger than my excuses. Those were enough to power me through day after day.

After all, we had started a swinery and not a 'whinery'. For some weird reason, I couldn't bring myself to complain because my mommy raised no whiner. But I had thoughts of quitting one too many times, though. I just fought the idea and didn't do it. However, to compensate for the exhaustion that I had felt, I took every chance to rest and recover in between, and to also daydream about everything that I desired to have in the future.

My first business partnership with my mom was a success because we were able to sell the pigs the moment they got bigger and were ready for slaughter. I kid you not but that was some crazy idea (for a ten-year-old at least!) that fortunately went well. Had I dared not ask my mom about the pigs, given in to overthinking, or allowed fear to take over me and just shoved the idea into oblivion, I wouldn't have known what I was capable of (hey, crossing highways and gathering slops were achievements worth celebrating). I wouldn't have experienced what was possible if I had just assumed rejection even before trying.

WAIS TIP #2: DO NOT BE AFRAID TO ASK QUESTIONS— EVEN THE ONES YOU THINK ARE 'DUMB' AND 'BASIC'

Humans are not mind readers. If we were created with telepathic abilities, we wouldn't need to regularly converse with people to express what we want. We wouldn't have to speak or act out what we feel, for the fulfilment of our daily needs. Chito and I could just look at each other in the eyes, instead, for a few seconds and we would already know exactly what to do or say. No words needed to be uttered. Not a sound.

But, newsflash, we were created with the ability to speak. We must make the most out of it at all costs—including the dreaded act of asking questions.

I have observed that one of the reasons why some people are hesitant to ask questions isn't because they do not have anything on their minds or because they are too shy to do so.

They do not ask for fear of looking stupid. As simple as that.

Every time I am in a conference or a group meeting and the fear of asking questions gets the best of me, I take a deep breath and remind myself that there are people in the room who are thinking about the same question but are also too nervous to ask it. More often than not, the question remains unanswered until a brave soul takes one for the team and does it. You'll notice how the room relaxes and conversations become clearer.

If the first technique doesn't work, I would again go back to how I usually was during my younger years—carefree and full of curiosity. Back then, it didn't bother me if I sounded stupid or annoying. I just knew I had a valid concern that needed to be acknowledged and the only way was to gather the courage and speak up. After all, I will never know if it's a 'yes', a 'no', or a 'maybe' if I never tried to ask.

Come to think of it, we may never have had partnerships with Amare La Cucina, Lime & Basil, and Jaytee's Classic restaurants had I allowed my fear of talking to people and asking questions to take over me. Because I knew that opportunities wouldn't come and wait for me all the time, I decided to make a move and asked the owners of each restaurant if I could partner with them. No 'ifs' and 'buts'. It was either a 'yes' or a 'no'.

On a side note, since we are talking about fear, I was once a brave soul back in the province but life happened and changed that when I started working. I transformed into this meek grown-up who is sometimes unsure of herself. When I became an actress (through Star Circle Quest, a reality-based talent competition) in Manila, it was only then that I was introduced to everything there was to know about the city life. During the process, I experienced a lot of discrimination and bullying and my insecurities got the best of me.

All these sad experiences had remoulded the once-courageous Neri into someone who lacked confidence. But, as you will find out in this book and my social media posts, I'm not the type to go down without a fight. So one day I decided to push back against every negative thing that was holding me back from living my best life. It wasn't by brute force, but I gave it a strong suckerpunch by constantly educating myself. (More about this on WAIS TIP #18 and Chapter 17.)

Because of the initial fear that I wanted and needed to conquer, I developed a strong desire to always keep improving and learning because I realized that I couldn't forever be scared of the world. The more I knew about something, a situation, or person I was scared of, the lesser and lesser it had its hold on me. And since I knew that practice makes progress, I'd constantly do it until the fear of whatever and whoever had no place in my mind any more.

Now, going back to the fear of asking questions, these are some of the things that I would do whenever I am a bit hesitant to shoot the question, most especially during classes or meetings (because let's admit it, being in a crowd sometimes feels intimidating):

1. **I jot** down all the questions that pop into my head so I don't forget (that's what my notebooks are for!). It doesn't matter if they sound ridiculous … I'm not going to ask them right away anyway.

2. **I listen** intently to check if the questions I have written were, in any way, already answered during the class or meeting. If they were, then I will cross them out, double-check the ones that are left, and decide if I still need them to be answered.

3. **I wait** until the end of the class or meeting, or if the speaker opens the floor to questions in the middle of the talk. Then, I take a deep breath and raise my hand for attention. There are some who—when the group is given the chance to ask—will open their mouths and talk right away. This can also work.

4. **I think** about my go-to motivational speaker or my favourite author. Or to be specific, I channel Audrey Hepburn's confidence when I feel that my mind is starting to overthink, eventually stopping me from asking questions. What would she do in this situation? Is she the kind of person to shrug it off when things don't get answered? Or will she push through until her thoughts are satisfied? Doing this helps me boost my morale. Since I have boundless imagination, I would momentarily act as if I were the woman I admired. In no time, I would feel the surge of confidence running through my veins.

5. **I know** I need clarification and I know I need help. Having these thoughts in mind pushes me to ask questions that will enable me to understand an idea better. This small act also shatters my ego and the illusion that I know everything there is to know.

6. **I speak** slowly and try not to eat my words because I tend to do it when I am excited about an idea. Doing this also gives my brain enough time to process my thoughts and articulate my ideas or questions well. If my nervousness gets the best of me, I pause for a few seconds, take a deep breath, and exhale. Then I try to ask the question again, clearly this time.

If I still find myself a little too hesitant to confidently fire that first question, or just simply try to strike up a conversation, I devote some time to practice. I've found out that though practice doesn't make one perfect right away, it sure makes progress for anyone who dares to take the first step.

I'd usually practice with Chito when he isn't too busy with work. We'd casually converse and ask random questions until I am comfortable with my thoughts and confident with the way I speak. I make sure, too, to not be offended when he corrects my grammar, diction, or the way I would ask a question because that's the only way I can become better.

And since I cannot master everything in one go, I'd often carve out an hour or so from my day just to practice and read more about it. Sometimes, when my day becomes too busy, I try to find more ways to squeeze it into my schedule which leads us to …

WAIS TIP #3: MAKE THE MOST OUT OF YOUR EARLY MORNINGS WHEN THE WORLD IS STILL ASLEEP

I am an early riser (as in the 4-a.m.-rise-and-shine type of person). I was inspired by Robert Iger, Walt Disney Company's CEO, who shared in one of his TED Talks that he gets up at 4.30 in the morning, seven days a week no matter where he is in the world. This way, he gets to start his day *waaaay* ahead of everyone else (which means fewer distractions and unnecessary conversations) to accomplish more tasks than he would have, had he awakened at around a later time.

So now, I try to wake up early in the morning, looking like a determined Neri who is excited to accomplish tasks and conquer the day. I call the gap—from the time I wake up until the second my children look for me—my 'ME Time' a.k.a. (M)orning (E)ssentials Time. Carved out of my busy day, I devote this pocket of time solely to myself before I divide the rest of the day for my family, school, hobbies, friends, and businesses. It's also the time when I can generate fresh ideas for my businesses and think of creative solutions to each problem we have at home and at work.

Comfort is good but, being inspired by the people who wake up early to be more productive, I realized that I had to go against what my mind and body would naturally do so I could own my day and not the other way around. Slowly, I would wake up at 4 in the morning. Sometimes 5 or 6, depending on how deep my sleep was. For as long as I wake up earlier than the rest of the world, I know I can still take charge of my day.

You'll usually find me in my office or anywhere in our home where there is a wide table that would fit my Morning Essentials (ME) such as a cup of tea or warm water in the morning. If I get my ME Time in the afternoon, it always comes with a glass of Coke Zero; a bag of chips, especially the local Filipino ones (I love them so much!), my laptop and calculator, my book of the month, and my set of favourite pens, highlighters, and notebooks.

I have different notebooks that are staples in my kit: dream notebook, to-do list notebook, and study notebook. I keep three separate ones because it helps me organize my thoughts well. And if I have an idea or something I want to go back to, I would know which notebook to get it from easily.

- The first of the three is my 'Dream' notebook. This is where I diligently jot down all my ideas, hopes, and dreams that I want to see, have, and experience one of these days. I write and describe in detail everything here because I know that I can never attain something or reach a place that I want to go to because I haven't envisioned them in my head yet. Let's say I want to have a rest house in Cebu (this is just an example, but who knows?!).
At this point, it will be hard for me to get there and make it happen if I haven't seen its final form in my head and plotted the way to get there. If I had just spoken about it once and not envisioned it daily, I would definitely be off-target. I even doubt I'll ever see that day when I would have a rest house in Cebu because it wasn't clearly pictured in my mind.

- Next is my 'To-Do List' notebook where I put everything that I need to accomplish in a day and the next few days so I don't forget. I jot down my top five priority tasks first, followed by those that can be done during the remaining hours of my day. I try to make it look like a checklist because ticking a box after I have finished a task gives me a certain high and it pushes me to accomplish more.

- Last is my 'Study' notebook which is a record of all my learnings from podcasts, instructional videos, online and offline classes, and even quotable quotes from the books I read and the people I meet and interact with. This is also where I record tips and tricks that I would pick up from different types of people I am able to observe during the day. It pays to pay attention to details that other people would overlook, you know.

Sometimes, when there's a bit more sun but the wind's still chilly, I'd go out to our garden and set up my ME Time there. Since we are based in Alfonso, a town popularly known for its cold climate, the refreshing daybreak breeze wakes me up and calms me down at the same time. Most of the time, I'd go for a walk at around 7.30 a.m. just to keep my body moving and my blood flowing.

I'd usually try to do at least 2,000 steps every morning. Walking keeps my mind relaxed and this, in turn, makes my mind the perfect sponge that can easily and fully absorb new ideas and more information. So, while at it, I would listen to a podcast or an online master class. Without realizing it, I have finished an episode or two filled with learnings just by exercising both my brain and body.

I also would walk around with a small notebook in my sling bag. It may seem silly to be carrying a notebook while walking unless you're an old-school detective of some sort. I mean, who usually does that? Well, I do! I never know when an idea would hit me so I have to be ready, at all times. You might ask, why don't I just type my ideas on my phone's notes app since it is easier that way? I manually write ideas down, even during my morning walk, because the mere act of writing helps me focus on the idea I'm trying to capture. Writing my thoughts on an actual paper also allows me to understand my thoughts better than when I type them on my phone.

On days when my thoughts would run faster than my hands could write, that's the only time that I'd whip out my phone and press the record button to document whatever idea I may have. Then, when I get home, I would eat a light breakfast and would spend half an hour or so transcribing or jotting down important points I have recorded. I would also spend a few minutes printing photos of whatever I was able to capture or my inspiration.

Oftentimes, I would be blessed with a couple more hours after my walk. When not reviewing my ideas, I would use the remaining hours for gardening. I love gardening so much that I allot time for this activity almost every day. At the same time I would either plant more seeds of my 'veggie of the month' or I would finally get to harvest fresh vegetables that my angels (house helpers) and I would, later on, prepare for lunch.

There's so much I could do with a little sacrifice called 'waking up at 4 a.m.' Of course, this isn't always the case. Don't get me wrong, we're humans, not robots. Uncontrollable happenings such as company meetings, late-night events that I have to attend, my kids not wanting to go to sleep early, and catching up on my online school assignments hinder me from sleeping early. This, in turn, makes me too tired and sleepy to wake up at 4 a.m. sharp all the time. On days like these, I go easy on myself and try my best to rise before the sun shines again the next day.

It takes discipline and I have to want it, to make it work. Whenever tempted to just throw all my efforts out the window, I remind myself of my strong desire to live a better life and stick to the mission. Otherwise, the 4-a.m.-habit will just be all for show.

Whenever I feel demotivated to wake up at this time, I would try to think of what I would get, if I moved earlier ahead of my household:

1. **More time for myself:** Since I cannot pour from an empty cup, waking up early allows me to fuel up for the day ahead through the various activities I would devote to my self-improvement or relaxation. I try to absorb as much information as I can—from books, podcasts, or news articles—around this time. Because when my children—Pia, Miggy, Cash, and my husband, aka my eldest child, Chito ☺—look for me, then I would have to refocus my attention and give them my time.

2. **More tasks accomplished:** Getting a head start helps me pace my tasks throughout the day. Because I have more time to do it in the morning, I don't have to rush from one task to get to the next in an instant! It saves me from procrastination and half-baked outputs. As a Wais Na Misis, I strive to give my family the best of me whenever I can and it only happens when I take my time.

3. **More energy to last me one full day:** I have noticed that I would have more than enough energy throughout the day whenever I spend thirty minutes to an hour just walking around the neighbourhood. I used to feel sleepy most of the time before, but now that I would consciously start my day with cardio and a little movement here and there, I seldom feel tired. But, if I do feel it in the middle of the day, I take power naps in between my activities as this helps me sustain my energy.

Sometimes, when Miggy would also wake up early he would join me during my walk or gardening. Yes, I love my ME Time but spending what remains of it with a loved one is such a refreshing and surprisingly energizing feeling, too.

I would take this time to expose Miggy to his immediate surroundings and teach him about literally anything he could think of. There would be days when he would ask me to teach him how to bake a cake or identify the plants in our garden. So I would gladly show him the plants that I would play with during my childhood like *gumamela* (hibiscus), *santan* (jungle geranium), and *makahiya* (mimosa pudica). My favourite days are the ones when he would tag along and help me gather our fresh vegetable harvest. This helps me teach him the value of hard work, how to be patient, and how to be grounded (literally and figuratively). It's not even 10 a.m. yet and I've already done most of my tasks before my children call out for me and I perform my mommy duties.

The early bird catches the worm and accomplishes more work indeed!

Maximize your morning and move, move, move before the sun shines. If you can't seem to figure out what to do in your early morning adventure, why don't you start with one of these?

1. Drink a glass of warm water.
2. Splash your face with cold water.
3. Start your day with a smile and a prayer.
4. Tell yourself five things you like about yourself. Declare what you believe in. Whatever you declare and accept, becomes your reality.
5. Say five things or name five people or experiences that you are thankful for.
6. If you can, walk outside in your garden or open the windows and inhale the fresh Philippine air (don't do this around 9 or 10 a.m. because you'll mostly be inhaling polluted air already) and exhale your worries and anxious thoughts.
7. Read at least five to ten pages of your favourite book. (HINT: *Wais Na Misis*)
8. Start a basic skincare routine. (Cleanser, toner, moisturizer, and sunscreen)
9. Enjoy and savour the silence for five to ten minutes. Savour the quiet. Inhale and exhale.
10. Eat your favourite breakfast and be mindful of chewing slowly and taking your time.
11. Write a to-do list for your next day before you sleep at night. Or you can also start planning the rest of your weekly or monthly calendar.
12. List down your goals for your family, career, personal life, business, and social life. The list doesn't have to be ideal or complete in one go.
13. Enjoy the time while preparing your family's breakfast. You can play an upbeat song as you cook their favourite morning meal.
14. Read up or watch something about an activity that sparks your passion. I love gardening and homemaking, so I usually watch videos or research more about those during my ME Time.

Chapter 2

From 5 to 500!

The knack for selling almost everything came naturally to me. I must have inherited it from my mom, the original Wais Na Misis. Growing up, I have always been quite close to my mom, so much so, that her selling skills must have been rubbed off on me. And one of the entrepreneurial lessons I learned from her as a child, and believe in till today, is ...

WAIS TIP #4: START WITH WHAT'S IN YOUR HANDS

I always knew I have to start somewhere and, like I said, it was okay if I started small.

This mindset that I applied on my piggery venture also came in handy when I had a crazy idea about selling our freshly uprooted *pechay* (Chinese cabbage) from my mom's vegetable garden. One morning I ran into my neighbour, a middle-aged woman, carrying a translucent plastic bag. In it was what looked like a fresh pig's foot from the wet market. In the middle of our small talk, I casually mentioned something along the lines of *'Ang sarap naman po ng tanghalian n'yo, parang nilaga!'* (Your boiled pork soup for lunch must be good!) My neighbour, who was dumbfounded, replied: *'Oo nga ano? Binili ko lang 'tong paa ng baboy pero 'di ko pa alam anong gagawin kong luto dito.'* (Oh, you're right! I just bought this pig's foot without an idea how I will cook it.) To which I quickly responded: *'Masarap po 'yan 'pag may pechay! Gusto n'yong bilhin yung pechay namin?'* (That goes well with pechay. We have one! Would you like to buy it?)

I am stifling a laugh as I write this. I promise you, that moment will forever be etched in my brain. How on earth did a ten-year-old Neri convince a neighbour, who was casually getting on with her day, to buy a Chinese cabbage? And, what in the world was I thinking when I tried to sell my mom's precious vegetables without her knowledge? She only got to know of the transaction when I showed her the first 5 pesos I had earned as a young and budding (but sneaky!) entrepreneur.

Haaay, Neri. But, I'm glad I did, though. And my mom was just as glad, too.

To cut the story short, I succeeded in convincing my neighbour to buy one huge pechay I had freshly harvested in our backyard vegetable garden. The transaction was so smooth and spontaneous that I remember I just handed her the vegetable without even putting it in a plastic bag or wrapping it with an old newspaper the way sellers usually do at the market.

Tell you what, what you have now is all you need. Work with what's in your hands. Search your immediate surroundings and you might just find something that can jumpstart a business. Do you have the smarts? Use it! Do you have the connections?

The idea? Build on it. The most important part here is that you have got to take the first step. This valuable lesson was what I needed to understand a few times, during my early college days, before I finally got to fully absorb what the lesson truly meant. This brings us to …

WAIS TIP #5: DON'T WAIT UNTIL THE CONDITIONS ARE FAVOURABLE BEFORE YOU TAKE THE FIRST STEP

Chances are, it will never be. And, more often than not, great opportunities will require you to hit the ground running. Gather the courage to say YES to opportunities and try to learn on the fly. As they often say, 'Don't knock it 'til you try it!'. Had I not dived headfirst; had I spent my time overthinking; and had I wasted my time trying to create an ideal scenario before I said yes to the opportunities, I wouldn't have won as second runner-up in the first beauty pageant I participated in and wouldn't have earned my first 500 pesos as a newbie local-television-host in Baguio.

It was 1997 and I was thirteen years old. We had just relocated from Subic to Baguio since my mom wanted me to study and spend the rest of our days there. During that time, my mom would always eagerly ask me to join beauty contests or audition for becoming an actress. I never knew what she saw in me but she was so persistent that she would bug me about it every now and then when the opportunities came. I guess she saw my being in show business as another opportunity to earn more money for myself and for my family at an early age. It was kind of an easy way for us to get out of poverty at that time.

One time, when I was about eighteen or nineteen years old, she handed me a newspaper clipping that had the details of a local beauty pageant. I thought she had already given up on that thought because I would always decline her every suggestion. But there she was again, excited, and urging me to join.

Upon realizing that it was indeed about a pageant, I panicked and almost froze in my seat. I didn't want to join the contest for two reasons: first, I wasn't used to the attention that contestants usually get, and second, I didn't want to wear a swimsuit. Period. You know how pageants are. There would always be a swimwear segment where contestants would parade around the stage with nothing but confidence and a few pieces of clothing on. I wasn't too fond of the idea because I wasn't quite confident, being almost stick-thin at 92 lbs. There was nothing for me to daringly flaunt for I didn't even feel pretty enough, to be honest.

What got me out of my seat and eventually convinced me to try and audition for the pageant was when my mom told me there was going to be a cash prize. I have forgotten how much it was but the words 'cash' and 'prize' were enough to inspire me that I had to give it a shot despite all my apprehensions. I remember my mom subtly doing reverse psychology by telling me to just go ahead and try auditioning because it wasn't that I would get shortlisted anyway. Maybe she had just wanted me to see for myself and get it over with, to satisfy her curiosity. Or like how I have previously mentioned—it may be one of her brilliant ideas for us to escape our situation. So, I went and auditioned. I was prepared to go home when, to my horror and surprise, the judges said I GOT IN!

Panic and excitement came rushing into my system the moment I was told I had gotten in. I was pretty ecstatic! After all, I knew it was going to be a new adventure but at the time I was panicking because I didn't know how I would tell my mom that I had passed the pageant screening I had initially been so hesitant about.

Fast forward to a few days and a couple of jittery hours later, I found myself owning the stage as I walked the runway like I had been participating in pageants my whole life. I guess I might have looked like I knew what I was doing because I have bagged most of the awards (Miss AVON, Face of ABS CBN Northern Luzon, and more that I can barely remember. I think I won almost all of them except the grand prize!) and even went home with a second runner-up title, beating the others who seemed to have more experience in pageantry than I had. Although, to be honest, the awards didn't matter much to me. All I cared about was I was able to bring home a small amount as a cash prize since the contest was over.

Whew! I thought I had survived my first and biggest wave. But I was dead wrong.

Little did I know that there would be an opportunity disguised as another intimidating wave waiting for its turn to crash into me. It was yet another panic-inducing moment that, looking back, I am thankful for. It came and pursued me once again despite my hesitation.

After I was awarded at the pageant, Sir Patrick, a manager from ABS CBN Baguio approached me and asked if I wanted to work for the said broadcasting company. In my head, I assumed he was offering me internship work because I hadn't even graduated from college then. So, a full-time job was off the table. Without giving it much thought, I said yes when he asked me to go to ABS CBN Baguio station, two days after that fateful coronation night.

I went there wearing my usual Baguio OOTD: jeans and a tube top with a jacket on. All the while, I thought I was going to do backstage production work since I was taking up AB Communications at the University of Baguio that time. It was but natural to do what I thought I would do. But I was dead wrong—yet again. When Sir Patrick asked me to take off my jacket, leave my inner top on, and have my makeup quickly done in the dressing room, I knew something was up.

Everything went by like a blur—it was so fast that I found myself holding a microphone and reading from a teleprompter. I WAS LIVE ON TV! Yes, all caps for shock and emphasis. I was that startled when I realized where I was standing in the middle of and what exactly was happening. All along, I had been reading scripts for a live regional variety show called ATIN TV. It was broadcast by ABS CBN Baguio and was shown all around Northern Luzon. And since I had no clue about what the entire scene was about, I kept messing up. Luckily some younger hosts were more experienced and gladly assisted me during the segment. They were so good at what they did, that they overshadowed my newbie mistakes and made the show almost flawless.

It wrapped up in an hour. I was left with sweaty hands and a head full of shame for I didn't know why I was put on that show, when I had zero experience in hosting. Recalling it now, as I type this, makes me cringe. I remember I kept apologizing to everyone, especially to Sir Patrick, for all the dead air and robotic hosting. He assured me that there was nothing to be sorry about because he knew it was my first time.

I believed him and thanked him for the opportunity. But, as I started to walk away, he stopped me in my tracks and told me to come back the next Sunday for another hosting gig. What had happened on my first day was still fresh in my mind, so I politely declined his offer. I told him I wasn't meant for that kind of work but I was comfortable working behind the camera and taking on work for behind the scenes.

I didn't know what Sir Patrick saw in me but he said, accompanied by a heave of sigh: 'Okay *sige, pero sayang ka may potential ka.*'(Okay sure, but you have the potential.) 'Here's your money for hosting today.' When I opened the envelope, I was so surprised to find 500 pesos in it. That time, that was a big amount. And for someone like me who wasn't born with a silver spoon in her mouth, 500 pesos was more than enough. So, I quickly asked: '*500 pesos para lang po sa ginawa ko sa isang oras?*' (500 pesos just for the hosting I did for one hour?) 'Yes,' he said, and that same amount will be given to me every Sunday after the show.

I took a step back and started mentally computing the amount I'd earn if I show up on all Sundays of the month. That would be 500 pesos multiplied by four Sundays so I would have a total of 2,000 pesos after a month. All I had to do to get that money was to host a television show for an hour. Scary, but I felt I could do it, so I went back to Sir Patrick and told him I would be back to host.

I owe it to my childhood experiences—my being a risk-taker in life and in business. Because I know that I will always have the chance to redeem myself and come back with a better battle plan I charge head-on. As long as I am breathing and I can still move my body and make my brain work, I know I still have the chance to make things right.

Even if it feels scary sometimes, I still try to go for it because I believe that God didn't give us the spirit of fear so why should we entertain that thought, right? Although, being fearless is entirely different from being reckless. In the former, you intentionally dive headfirst with a positive goal in mind regardless of the situation—you know when to back out or slow down. The latter is just being careless—you have no sense of danger and even the slightest consideration in your actions. You just do what pleases you at that moment.

Now that it's clear, allow me to challenge you with this: *Huwag ka matakot kasi kasama natin parati si Lord. Kung hindi mo susubukan, paano mo malalaman? Kung hindi ngayon, kailan?* (Don't be scared because God is always by our side. If you're not going to try it, how would you know the outcome? If not now, when?)

WAIS TIP #6: IF AT FIRST YOU DON'T SUCCEED, YOU CAN ALWAYS TRY AGAIN AND COME BACK BETTER AND STRONGER

VICTORY LOVES PREPARATION, I've seen this phrase quoted one too many times in movies and speeches. It has also been reposted quite a lot on random social media posts.

I believe, this phrase also applies to this part of my story.

Remember the hosting stint I had agreed to come back to? Well, I did but I made sure I was well-equipped when I did. I've known it too well that in order to succeed in the new path I was trying to take, I had to come prepared and in full battle gear.

Since I accepted the hosting offer that aired on a Sunday, I maximized the remaining days of the week until the next Sunday by studying everything I needed to know about television hosting. I watched ATIN TV replays and studied how the hosts would normally act in front of the camera. I took notes of their body language, bubbly demeanor, and voice modulation. I also intently observed how they would deliver their lines without looking at the teleprompter all the time.

I was so determined to come back as a better host than the first time they had seen me, that I had devoted most of my days practising until I felt confident in my hosting as if it was second nature to me.

I stepped in front of the camera the next Sunday with my A game and the rest, as they say, was history. Soon enough I found myself hosting more shows. I even became the face of ABS CBN regional because of it. There would be times when they would assign me to cover concerts, like the ones of Side A, a well-known Filipino band, and they let me have exclusive interviews with various Filipino artists. In hindsight, it would have been a hilarious story to recount if I had interviewed Parokya ni Edgar (a Filipino pop-rock band of which my husband, Chito, is the main vocalist).

Anyway, so in a year, by God's grace, I was able to experience firsthand what other communications students my age would only dream of and hear about in schools.

Because I had prepared the second time I was given the opportunity, the job I thought I had no business in and I once dreaded, turned out to be a blessing for me.

The same thing happened when I started to take an interest in putting up a business during my show-business days. Chito and I were already in a relationship at the time we decided to franchise a milk tea business. Since I was focused on acting, I didn't have enough know-how to make our first business venture a success. This failure prompted me to learn more about the nitty-gritty of the industry so that when I try again, I would be prepared and won't get swallowed by the waves because I now know how to ride them.

I always say to anyone who would ask me why I keep on trying new business ventures with so much courage and grit as if I didn't fail on the first try: *'Walang mangyayari kung hindi mo susubukan. Kung madapa ka man at least sinubukan mo at natuto ka.'* (Nothing's going to happen if you don't try. If you fail, at least you tried and you learned from it.)

Chapter 3

When Life Throws You Lemons, Sell 'em!

I used to wonder what my God-gifted skill was. It wasn't singing, dancing, oh, and definitely not painting. Let's leave the arts to my children—Pia and Miggy (they are super awesome artists by the way!). I thought long and hard about what was that one thing that got me most excited and what I effortlessly excelled at since I was a child.

I could barely think of any; until I remembered I had so much fun talking to people, particularly adults like moms and professionals from whom I was able to absorb much wisdom. It was also easy for me to turn the casual conversations into opportunities for me to either sell what I had in my backyard or convince them to buy whatever I had in my hands at the moment. I would also have creative ideas about how I could effectively sell my mom's goods. These ideas, however crazy, were mainstays in my mind. I could just as easily pull them up, whenever I needed a strategy for my mom's new small business as I would a punchline.

Because of all of these, I truly believe that God has blessed me with marketing and entrepreneurial skills. It is as valuable as any motor or visual skills that most of us are quite familiar with. It isn't the run-of-the-mill kind of a talent, my being a natural marketer and entrepreneur, to say the least; but it sure took my and my family's life to heights far better than what I had imagined as a young girl in Subic and Baguio.

Growing up, I had plenty of business ideas sprouting in my head from time to time. But, because I lacked the knowledge, wisdom, money, and experience to begin working on one, the ideas remained in my head until I encountered an opportunity to make them come to life.

These business opportunities usually would sprout from some random conversations with my neighbours or from mere observations I've had during the day.

WAIS TIP #7: DO YOUR RESEARCH, OBSERVE THE DYNAMICS OF YOUR COMMUNITY

No matter how good or how afforable you think your product is, if it doesn't answer your immediate community's needs or if it doesn't catch their interest, you might have a bit of a hard time selling them. I have learned this during my younger years as my mom's errand girl. She would often ask me to visit the nearby sari-sari store to buy vegetables, soda, cigarettes, or our day's snack on credit—just because I was the youngest child who was always left at home. On my way to the store and back, I would catch a glimpse of the daily lives my neighbourhood would often lead. I would see what they mostly consume, the kinds of brands they patronize, and their personal preferences when it comes to their basic needs such as clothes and food. I would take note of all of them.

I know you might think that these thoughts were bordering on impossible to occur for a child like me. But believe me when I say that these came naturally to me. Sure, I also did have some daydreams and random thoughts that were typical of a child, but they didn't come as often as the entrepreneurial ones. I guess I really must have been wired differently and it came in handy when my mom needed help with every small business she would put up.

Casually striking up conversations with people has become my habit growing up. As a teen and eventually an adult, I would make it a point to spend a few minutes of my time speaking with a local vendor or a business owner who have been in the industry for quite some time. This allows me to get a feel of the market and pick their brains at the same time. As much as I love learning from books, nothing beats the lessons I often get from people who are deep in the field. If you can learn from both, better!

Many businesses, if not all, are born out of a need. I have mentioned this in interviews and I will say this again: 'Whatever challenges you have at home can spark a business idea.' Now, let me tell you that these kinds of information can only stem from casual and consistent conversations with the experts. So you better start talking to them when you get a chance!

Take for example this one instance in Subic. When I found out that our neighbourhood at that time was fond of the dishes made from pork and beef, I then went up to my mom and asked if we could raise pigs for slaughter as our first money-making venture based on my observations. When I made my first vegetable sale, I told my mom that our neighbours love vegetables, and so we started growing our own mini-backyard vegetable garden. We benefited from this, too, because we love vegetables just as much and we always have a vegetable dish on our table because they are affordable.

Back in Baguio, my mom sold barbecue because street food was always in demand. On days when our sales were low, I would ask my pretty older sister to sit beside me and help me get every passer-by's attention so we could attract more customers and make more sales. Of course, that wasn't just a random decision on my end. I saw how there was a fair number of people around the area and I thought having a pretty face near our barbecue stand would catch their attention and boost our sales. And it sure did!

Wanting to test my 'pretty sister as endorser' strategy, we had set up a table in Mines View Park, Baguio one summer. I saw the way it was packed with visitors every year because this iconic park is well-known for attracting large groups of vacationers from all over the Philippines. They come to Baguio, all the way from different parts of the country, just to enjoy the chill mountainside breeze under the warm summer sun.

My sister and I decided to settle at a spot from where most of the tourists would pass by. By doing this, the tourists could quickly catch a glimpse of my pretty sister whom I asked to sit by the front of our table. Come to think of it, I already had an idea to use 'influencers' and 'endorsers' even when it wasn't so much of a thing! See? Don't knock 'em 'til you try 'em!

In no time, we were able to sell a whole lot of barbecue, grilled corn on the cob, and grilled dried squid. My mom's simple business idea became our very first 'family business', and it turned out to be a successful one at that. We went home with more or less PhP 20,000 gross income.

My mom, seeing how big an amount it was, might have become a little too excited and bought an entire sofa-set right away. Our hard-earned money wasn't maximized and used in away to generate more money—something the entrepreneurs around usually do, so we were back to square one. I didn't know any better at the time so I thought it was normal and it was exactly how we should be celebrating after every successful sale. Unfortunately, I had absorbed this mindset until Chito helped me unlearn this during the course of our relationship.

What had happened also prompted me to constantly remind people of . . .

WAIS TIP #8: DON'T SPEND ALL YOUR EARNINGS IN ONE GO

I rested on the idea that my money will never run out but my days to spend it will. When I earned one of my first few salaries as an actress, I blew it. I mean, no one guided me on how to properly handle money. And we barely got while growing up. So, when I had the chance to earn a lot during my acting days, I splurged on myself because that was the first time I was ever able to afford high-ticket items and experiences for myself.

It was a good experience and I don't regret it. But, it sure had put a huge dent in my financial stability. Where do you think I would learn how to manage my finances wisely? It wasn't from my neighbours, surely.

So, I thank God that He gave me Chito. If it weren't for his navigations, I would have had a hard time managing my money smartly and correctly. He has taught me everything I needed to know about money. One important thing that I have learned from him was to never spend all my hard-earned cash in one go.

Let's say, for example, we were able to earn PhP 20,000 from selling food in Mines View Park. Our smart move could have been: saving 10,000, keeping aside 5,000 to use for our family's daily expenses, and using the remaining 5,000 as capital for our next business idea. That or we could have used it to buy more grilled street foods that we could sell in the next few days. That would have been sustainable.

The same principle applies when you are planning to start a business. Start small and go slow. If you were like me who didn't have extra cash to spare on the first try, take caution. It would be wise to allot a small or manageable amount first. I had to learn this the hard way during my first milk tea franchise and pharmacy business. Because I had minimal money management skills at that time, I'd spent most of my earnings on both businesses and lost in the end, without even being able to earn a single centavo. I had even lost about PhP 500,000 to PhP 600,000!!!

At that time, I had in my head that if my friends could successfully franchise a business then I could do it, too, without realizing that getting into it would entail deeper research and planning.

Moving forward, resisting the urge to pour all my resources into one basket is a precautionary measure I had learned the hard way. If there's one key takeaway from this book that you should always keep in mind, may it be this: never pour out all your money because if your first try fails, you will still have enough money to use for the next venture. You won't end up with a depleted bank account.

It's also been one of my healthy habits to check my financial capabilities at the time when I have plans to buy or invest in a new business. Like for our resthouse in Baguio, I initially checked if I could afford it with the allotted budget that I had. When I knew I was running a bit short, I asked Chito if he wanted to invest in this idea of a resthouse so we could both own it.

Now, you may wonder why we would do this as a couple when we have a joint bank account to use anyway? It is because even if we have a shared pool of money as a couple, we also like to keep the ones that we earn on our own, in separate bank accounts and use them for our different investments.

Given this, I wouldn't have bought the resthouse if I didn't have enough money in the bank and had Chito not agreed to invest in it with me. I had big dreams, but I knew that reality's always there to keep us, our goals, and sometimes our egos in check so we don't go overboard.

WAIS TIP #9: ANSWER A NEED AND MONEY WILL FOLLOW

I was always asked how did I start selling and how did I become a full-fledged entrepreneur. Counting all the years that I have tried to make money out of selling casually, I could say I have been doing it since I was younger. But it was only during the COVID-19 pandemic that my image and my credentials as a businesswoman were cemented. It was a 180-degree turn from being Neri the actress to Neri the entrepreneur.

I didn't always have the best ideas. But the ones that I believe answered a need became successful. It even gave birth to more ideas and business opportunities. Of course, our goal for investing in a business and selling is to earn. But, over time, I have come to realise that focusing on being a brand or a business that fulfils some of the community's needs is one of the surefire ways of making a business succeed, which eventually helps the brand earn more money. I believe this is a better move than just focusing on earning money right away, regardless of whether the people within the brand's immediate circle are benefiting from it or not.

The *ukayan* (thrift shop), that is now owned by my bestfriend, Ninang Mace, was born out of my need for affordable fashion. I loved dressing up as a child and I grew up buying my clothes from a nearby ukay-ukay in Baguio. I still wanted to dress up but I didn't want to spend too much on clothes, so I had put this up for other people to have affordable options.

When I established my brand Very Neri which carried bed sheets, accessories, sleepwear, and more fashionable clothes in collaboration with the Saturday Dress brand, I had the needs of a busy homemaker in mind. The need for a one-stop online shop where she can browse through and get her needs and wants fulfilled without any hassle. As for 'Neri's Not-So-Secret Garden', it was the culmination of everything that I had ever dreamt of when I was younger. I wanted to have a cafe, a restaurant, and just a place where everyone could hang out and have a good time. It also answered the need for good comfort food. That was exactly what all we offered.

Serving other people's needs was also at the core of my Gourmet Tuyo brand. I didn't imagine for it to become as successful as it is now. In all honesty, I didn't have the thought of generating hundreds and thousands of pesos from selling it during the time I was perfecting its recipe in my home kitchen. Before the *tuyo* (gourmet dried fish) brand blew up, all I wanted was to whip up a mouth-watering gourmet tuyo for my brother-in-law who loves it. That was it, that was just my need–to serve good food and make my every house-guest happy.

When I visited my in-laws' house, I saw how they had a lot of gourmet tuyo in the kitchen. I was so inspired by the many variants there are, that I researched about the best gourmet tuyo recipes on the internet as soon as I got back home. When I found a few of those, I tried my hand at them so I could check which ones suit my taste the best. It's funny, though, when I look back on that day; because, before that, I had never tasted an authentic gourmet tuyo in my life. Since I had no point of comparison, I left it in the fridge for storage as soon as it was bottled. I never thought of offering it for anyone to taste test. I wasn't even hoping anyone would dare taste it. So it went straight to the back of my refrigerator.

I had forgotten it existed until a few weeks after when our friends, who visited our home in the morning, decided to extend their stay to chill and drink so they could enjoy the chilly weather even more. I didn't join them because I had planned to sleep at around 9 p.m. Come midnight, my friends felt hungry. Since I, their official cook, was already fast asleep, they just went to the kitchen to fix themselves their own meals. While looking for more food to prepare, they saw a bottle of unlabeled gourmet tuyo sitting at the back of our refrigerator, and decided to try it.

To my surprise, they all loved it and they even asked if I could make more for them. But, the silly old me didn't take note of the first recipe so I had to do it again. This time I diligently took notes and recorded every step I took so my team and I could easily replicate it whenever my friends would order from me. By order, I mean, I only did it for them. It wasn't commercially available at that time as it was more of a hobby and a friends-only deal.

I was also at that point where I was so hesitant to risk another season of my life, plus my hard-earned money, for business. I have had my fair share of failed businesses; it was but normal to feel unsure about the whole situation.

I wasn't ready to try creating a product and selling it again but my market was.

Through the demands from my immediate circle and other people who had heard about it, I found out that the need for a local savoury and affordable gourmet tuyo was only increasing. One minute I was shoving an unlabeled gourmet tuyo bottle at the back of our refrigerator and the next minute I was pulling it out and diligently reproducing a better version for customers and bazaar organizers who had expressed their interest in my product. I found myself at a local bazaar, with only a capital of PhP 3,000. In less than two hours, I was able to sell all 150 bottles of my gourmet tuyo. And in no time, my PhP 3,000 became PhP15,000 and then PhP 25,000. Eventually, I was earning PhP 100,000 which grew to PhP 250,000, and then to PhP 500,000. I was able to reach almost a million pesos in total earnings. All of these earnings were through selling gourmet tuyo.

Of course, this amount wouldn't have been possible if not for the grace of God, the patronage of my new and repeated customers, as well as the dedication and hard work of my production team. Everything worked out in the end. All I needed to do was to take the leap of faith and allow everything to take its natural course.

When life throws lemons at you, don't be afraid to catch them and sell them!

Now that you know my journey as an entrepreneur and hopefully my stories may have sparked ideas in your creative brains, your next question might probably be: how to make sure that your ideas are worth committing to.

Here are some of the lessons I have learned, through trial and error, before starting a business. Please remember that these are from my journey as an entrepreneur. Some points here may or may not apply to you. Although some of these, you may also tweak according to your current situation. I am glad to share the questions that I always ask myself before committing to a new business. I am hoping that you'll somehow pick a thing or two from my triumphs and my booboos. Let me introduce you to the five Ws and one H.

1. **WHAT IS MY PRODUCT?**

   What is it that I am trying to sell? Is it a tangible item or is it a service? These are the initial questions I always ask myself. After all, my product should be as specific as I could make it, so my customers won't get confused. As soon as I figure out what I want to sell, I make sure that the product gets through a thorough research and development process before I put it out in the world. Days leading to its launch, I must have had it already tested by random people from within and outside of my circle, most especially if it's a food product. Apart from the taste, safety and sanitation are my top concerns for such a product. As for non-perishable items like bedsheets and clothes, I would usually do stress tests on my own household to see if the product would last for longer periods.

2. **WHY AM I STARTING THIS BUSINESS?**

   This goes hand in hand with my question, 'What is my passion and what are my skills?'. The things that excite me the most, such as gardening, bargain hunting, and cooking, fall under this category. Try to define and list down yours. But always remember that the things you are passionate about, should also align with your existing skills. For example, if your passion revolves around food or putting up a chain of restaurants and, sadly, kitchen work is not among your skillsets or you are not fond of cooking at all, then your idea might not work well. So, an added tip is that you should try to find something in which both aspects critical to a service are aligned for your business to flourish.

   Also, remember not to pursue the business idea if you want to have a franchise or a brand just for the heck of it. Never do it because it is what's in at the moment or your friends are doing and have been successful. Do it because it sparks your joy and creativity, and it also serves your community. Also, going back to *WAIS TIP #9*, it would be a huge plus if your business or your product would answer a need.

3. **WHERE IS MY INITIAL MONEY GOING TO COME FROM?**

This is the part where I usually take my time and list down all my resources before I even try to decide if I would push through with a business idea or not. I double-check if my capital would come from my savings or from a portion of my earnings (My VERY NERI starting capital of PhP 100,000 came from some of my sales from NERI's Gourmet Tuyo). I try not to take loans from the bank or make deals with loan sharks so even in case the business doesn't fly, I won't have a hard time moving on to the next idea because my credit record is clear. So, I say save up save up save up for your dream business! It's easier and safer that way.

4. **WHO ARE THE KEY PEOPLE IN MY BUSINESS?**

Part of my business planning is listing down the number of staff I would be needing. I know that I cannot do it alone so might as well take into consideration the team I will need to build at the outset. This makes it easier for me to determine my working budget as well as the work delegation strategies.

5. **WHEN and WHERE DO I PLAN TO LAUNCH IT?**

The launch date is very crucial as this determines the flow of my production calendar. I do not want to put out half-baked products and neither should you. I always plot my launch date and venue (whether a physical location or happening online) early on the calendar because it helps me create my marketing plans.

Of course, apart from the production, I also need to strategize its introduction to the market as it plays a very important role. Whenever I plan to launch or sell something, I do my market research through social media, too. This is the time that I post about the product or the investment and ask my followers what they think about it. Their opinions matter and I want to take into consideration their comments and suggestions before I release anything from my brands.

6. HOW MUCH AM I WILLING TO SPEND?

The amount I allocate for a new business is usually big enough to cover the initial expenses but conservative enough for me to easily let go, should the business fail. Also, remember *WAIS TIP #8* so you don't use up all your savings for one product or idea.

WAIS TIP #10: NEVER BE ASHAMED OF YOUR BUSINESS IDEAS NO MATTER HOW SMALL THEY MAY SEEM

When I launched Neri's Gourmet Tuyo, random people looked down on me. They even commented that I resorted to selling tuyo just because I didn't become famous and successful as an actress. Some even laughed at me because I am the wife of Chito Miranda, the vocalist of a well-known Filipino band, and yet here I am selling bottled smelly dried fish drenched in olive oil.

The joke's on them because selling is in my DNA. I grew up in an environment where I had no other choice but to think of a hundred ways to earn an honest living and to peddle whatever my mom and I could get our hands on. It's what I was conditioned to do, especially in situations where our family's necessities and comfort are at stake.

Let me take you back once again to my younger years so you understand better what I'm talking about. As I've mentioned several times now, growing up, I had been accustomed to finding new ways to earn at every chance I get.

My dad may have had a fairly decent job abroad as an Overseas Filipino Worker (OFW) but whatever amount he would send, my mom did her best to budget it and make it work for a family of five. That was how challenging our situation was. Because of this, my young mind had developed a survival mode that switched on each time I would see that we were running out of food or money. This mode kept me alive. It pushed me to find more ways to earn whenever the inevitable happened. It inspired me to strive harder so I can help upgrade our lives. We were living an okay life, we weren't dirt-poor, but I aspired for it to become better.

From elementary to high school I sold all kinds of goods. From pechay, pigs, and barbecue, to corn on the cob and dried squid.

In college, I would use my break time to sell my mom's home-cooked rice meals to a nearby compound filled with office buildings to make more money. It was tiring and tough because I had to travel from my school to the office compound and back again just to sell hot meals during lunchtime.

My only point is that I wasn't ashamed of selling all sorts of stuff back then, so why should I be ashamed of it now? As long as I am earning an honest living for myself and my family, I am not exploiting anyone, and I am not trying to make money to support my vices or irrational extravagances then I don't see anything wrong with me selling anything. I've said this in the interviews and I'll say it again: 'You will not be able to feed your family if you will be ashamed of selling. People who laugh at you—because you are ONLY a seller—DO NOT matter.'

Selling is a noble source of livelihood. Anyone who makes fun of you because of what you do, could only dream of earning a fortune that you are earning by doing what you love. So don't mind the naysayers and just keep on doing your best! YOU ARE DOING GREAT!

Chapter 4

'Momma Now Knows . . . Better'

I am a mother first before an entrepreneur, a brand endorser, or Wais Na Misis. My family comes first before anything else—even important meetings. However, as my family grows, so do my businesses. I must admit, there are days when I try to do *Everything Everywhere All At Once* (sounds familiar? hehe), it definitely takes a huge toll on my physical, mental, and spiritual health. At times, I am tempted to drop everything to breathe and recover but I can't do that always, can I?

What's a mompreneur like me to do then?

WAIS TIP #11: LEARN HOW TO PRIORITIZE

Just like my daily schedule, where I rank the tasks depending on their urgency, I also prioritize when it comes to my personal and work life. As I have said, my family comes first so obviously—Chito, Pia, Miggy, and Cash are the top four names that get most of my attention. Anything that concerns them is non-negotiable. For example, if I am in a staff meeting and Miggy calls for me for whatever reason, I would politely excuse myself from the said meeting to attend to my son. Of course, it also helped that I have established this unwritten rule within my team because they already know why I did what I did.

When I am faced with new clients or brands, I would inform them at the start of our negotiations about my priorities. Thank goodness they always understand so I didn't have a hard time excusing myself or rearranging schedules to fit my family's needs.

Work will always be there, but my kids won't stay this young forever. This is also a crucial time for me to be present in their formative years.

I grew up with just my mom present during the most important years of my life because my dad was either working abroad or spending time with his friends when he was back home. Because of this, I had only learned a lot of street smarts from my mom because it was her who was with me almost the entire time.

It helps that I list everything that I need to do the night before, so I don't miss out on anything when I am on my mommy and work duties. While doing groceries, I usually have a checklist ready so when I head to the wet market, I already have an idea of where to go and what all to put in my cart. This saves me time and unnecessary spending.

Remember *WAIS TIP #3*? If all else fails, I do my best to wake up super early to catch up on work because the moment my household wakes up, the bulk of my day is left and can be dedicated to them. My early mornings are for relaxation, research, answering e-mails, solving business-related problems, and reviewing how my brands have recently performed. Sticking to this kind of routine helps me maintain a healthy and balanced work and mom life.

WAIS TIP #12: LEARN HOW TO DELEGATE

For many reasons, we, moms, tend to always multitask. I feel a sense of accomplishment whenever I am able to do a lot of things in one day. I'd also like to believe it's one of our superpowers to juggle multiple things and accomplish them before the day ends. It's good if you can do that, I salute you! However, as I grew older and wiser, I have realized that this kind of take, on my kind of mompreneur life, has its downsides, too. One of which is the risk of putting out a mediocre job. Who wants to eat half-baked bread? Nobody.

Because I know that stretching myself too thin will do my family and businesses more harm than good, and so I have embraced the art of delegating. It felt weird at first, having to let go of the many responsibilities I once carried. But, as I did it continually, my mind and body became used to not having to do everything all the time. Since my family and businesses are continuously growing, I have assigned tasks that I once handled to the rest of my team. I have also hired people who I think know more than I do when it comes to a certain area of the business. This resulted in better output, an efficient work system, and more trust among my staff members.

WAIS TIP #13: USE SOCIAL MEDIA AND THE INTERNET TO YOUR ADVANTAGE

We are in the digital era. Social media and the internet are two things that the current generation will not live without. Since it's become a staple in our daily lives, the mere awareness of how it can be used differently is an advantage. Typically, we'd use social media to post about our day-to-day lives—the food we eat, the clothes we wear, the places we go to, and even the most mundane things we post, for ourselves and for the people who choose to follow us. With the awareness around the dangers of consuming too much of social media platforms (for example, the fear of missing out (FOMO) and unhealthy comparison), I now make it a point to intently just use Instagram or Facebook for research and business promotion. I don't linger and lurk in it for more than an hour if I am not doing any research. Also, I only follow the ones whom I know I can learn from. This way, my feed rarely contains any non-essential information that would suck me into the gossip blackhole, eventually wasting my precious time.

WAIS TIP #14: REMEMBER THAT ASKING FOR HELP IS NOT A SIGN OF WEAKNESS

I am aware that as much as I would like to be one, I am no superwoman. At any given time, when my system becomes overloaded, I will surely break down and overheat. This is why I do not shy away from asking for help, most especially from God, through prayers, and my family as well. This same act, for me, is more of an empowering trait than a weakness if you use it correctly and if you look at it from an egoless perspective. I have noticed that being open about seeking help creates a certain bond among family members and my team at work (see *WAIS TIP #12*). I was even surprised that people are so much more than willing to help because, apart from having the task done, it makes them happy and fulfilled while doing it. Win-win!

Also, if not for the courage to ask for help from Chito, I would still be the same Neri who would splurge all her money on random useless stuff that tickled my fancy. We got married and I barely had any money left in my bank account. That was how messed up my financial status was. My being Wais Na Misis now is so much different from the old Neri who used to spend most of her earnings thinking that she'll probably have more in the next few days because of her job as an actress. I was living the YOLO (You Only Live Once) principle until I asked Chito to teach me his equally WAIS ways of handling money.

Asking for help won't make you any less of a person. If anything, it will bust your ego but it will increase your knowledge and wisdom, remember that.

Chapter 5

Financial Management CHITOrial

Contrary to popular belief, Chito is the more disciplined and educated when it comes to handling money. I am simply his apprentice who constantly learns from him every day. It may sound unbelievable, to those who do not personally know us, because he appears to be a happy-go-lucky rockstar who can splurge all his earnings whenever he wants to. But, believe me, without him, I wouldn't be the kind of Wais Na Misis that I am today.

This part of my book is a tribute to the awesome guy I am blessed to call my husband. God must have seen me still struggling financially even when I worked as an actress. I was earning just enough but I was spending as if I made a lot. Perhaps I was also on the brink of blowing up God's purpose for me because of my negligence, that's why He sent Chito my way to be my mentor, my best friend, and my partner in life and in business.

During the course of our relationship, I saw how he managed his hard-earned money well. I saw all of the fruits of his discipline and hard work, too! It was so impressive that I told him I wanted to have the same lifestyle and financial stability that he has. This next tip may vary because we obviously have different men as husbands, all of which have different personalities. But, in any case when your husband or partner, the person you've sworn to live life with for better or for worse and for richer or for poorer, offers you reliable financial management advice, please don't take it as an attack on your personality. He loves you and he just wants the best for you and your family.

WAIS TIP #15: LISTEN TO YOUR HUSBAND WHEN HE TEACHES YOU HOW TO MANAGE YOUR MONEY. DON'T TAKE OFFENSE. HE MEANS WELL AND HE WANTS TO SEE YOU SUCCEED

Here are my favourite tips and tricks (some I may have briefly mentioned in the previous WAIS TIPS and chapters) I've learned from Chito and that learning has helped me in my journey to becoming Wais Na Misis:

1. **NEVER SPEND MONEY YOU DO NOT HAVE**
   As previously mentioned, I used to rely on the idea that I will always have money as long as I am working and I have work lined up in the next few months or years. Well, that is partly true. Because the reality is, yes, I may have secured contracts or schedules that will make me financially stable. But, Chito told me that as long as the agreed money hasn't reached my hands or any of my bank accounts, I don't have the right to assume ownership of it. Whatever I have in my accounts and my wallet, is the only money I can wisely spend.
   Chito also emphasized that I should never get into the habit of borrowing money or using credit cards for all transactions. Because, no matter how convenient and enticing that may appear, it is still not the money that I have.

2. **SPEND-PROOF YOUR MONEY**
   As the adage goes, never put all your eggs in one basket. For example, you earn PhP 57,000. Distribute and deposit PhP 50,000 to different bank accounts and make sure that you will have a hard time accessing your money any time you wish to. You can put your savings in a time deposit or a passbook account or invest it. Just leave a few thousand or hundreds in your ATM or wallet for your daily needs. Out of sight, out of mind.

3. **SPEND ON THINGS, EXPERIENCES, OR PROPERTIES THAT WILL CREATE MORE MONEY FOR YOU**
   I used to spend on things that I liked and that brought me happiness, but nothing more beyond that. It wasn't until Chito told me about this new way of spending when I realized it was also possible to buy things that aren't just mere objects. I could

also buy those that can make more money for me like properties, bakery equipment, condominiums, rest houses, and people's skills too. The list is endless. The moment I got into that mindset, all my expenses became more intentional and practical.

4. **LIVE BELOW YOUR MEANS**

    Would you believe that when Chito started earning as a singer, he didn't buy an extravagant vehicle as his main transportation for his gigs? I used to assume that because of his rockstar status, he would have chosen a Hummer or a Harley Davidson, or a Vespa to complement his work and lifestyle. But, when we started going out, I saw that he drove a humble, old, white Honda Jazz. Later on, I found out that the only reason he had that car was he only needed it to get him from one place to another for work. Nothing more, nothing less. Sure, he could easily buy himself whatever car he desired but he decided to spend the money he had on investments, insurance, and properties. After all, the value of the car will eventually depreciate over time while his investments appreciate.

5. **SAVE BEFORE YOU SPEND**

    Chito taught me that for instance, I earned PhP 25,000 today. What I should firstly do is save PhP 20,000 from it and leave the PhP 5,000 in my wallet or ATM account for my daily expenses. This way, I will only have a certain budget for the month or the week that I can work around with. Doing this will also prevent me from overspending or buying stuff that I don't need. He is always quick to remind me that it doesn't matter how huge or small my salary or talent fee is, it's how I handle the money. Whether I have PhP 1,000 or PhP 1M in my bank account, if I don't know how to manage it well, it will all disappear in a snap.

6. **CREATE MULTIPLE SOURCES OF INCOME**

    It's good to own a business, work as a freelancer, or have a stable job. But I realized that for me, it is better if I can manage to have more than one source of income. Because if and when my main source of income becomes unavailable or unstable, I would still have other income streams to get me by. Also, doing this enables me to earn more and save more.

So, ask yourself, what are the other sources of income that you can think of apart from the one that you have now? Or, do you have another skillset that can make extra money for you while you do your main job?

7. **ENCOURAGE YOUR PARTNER TO HAVE HER OWN SOURCE OF INCOME**
(This one is not a requirement and situations may vary)
Chito would always encourage me to pursue business ideas or other means of acquiring more money so I can earn more for myself. Not that he didn't want to provide for the family any more, he still does and he will never stop, but he encourages me so that whenever I see something that I liked, I can easily buy it for myself because I have my own money at hand.

Many still believe in stereotypes that say men are designed to be providers. But I say that women, wives, and mothers can earn and have the right to our own income and means of livelihood just as much. Or otherwise, if you are given a budget or a personal allowance, make sure to save some for when you want to treat yourself.

I remember there was one time I wanted to buy a dainty dessert tray that I had found online. I wanted it so bad that I had almost lost sleep over it. When I couldn't take it any more, I told Chito I wanted to buy it, but I didn't have enough money to do so. He was supportive and more than willing to get it for me but not without asking me a lot of questions. It was as if I was already defending my MBA thesis.

He asked me to justify why I wanted to have it and where the item will be used. I probably got a bit tired and kind of irritated at his questions, so I decided not to push through with the transaction any more no matter how much I wanted the item. That was a learning moment for me.

After that incident, I strived to have my own source of income so I could responsibly buy or do whatever I wanted without being answerable to anyone but myself.

PART 2: Life Moves in Mysterious WAIS

Chapter 6

Hope

As my mom's default errand girl growing up in the provinces of Subic and Baguio, I was well aware that Hope was a famous cigarette brand. It was the same brand that my mom would often ask me to get a few sticks or a pack of from the nearby sari-sari store, and have it listed on credit. That was all I knew of the word. I didn't know that it meant something deeper than the intoxicating smell of tobacco it left on my mom's fingers or the smell that remains in the fibers of her clothes even after thorough washing.

I didn't know that it would be the same word that would help me survive my childhood and adolescent years. HOPE. What an unpretentious four-letter word. If I didn't have it, little Neri may not have survived her version of 'a series of unfortunate events'. Hope has kept me going for the past forty years of my life. (Yes, that is my real age!)

At this point, you may be wondering what events I am talking about. Let's rewind my story to some years back.

When I entered the exciting but crazy adolescent stage, I also started wearing flowy skirts that were just bought from the ukay-ukay. We didn't have much back then, so the thrift store was our go-to destination for our fashion needs.

Wearing flowy and colourful skirts made me feel like a princess. The cheap but cute, brightly coloured headbands that my mom would get me from the nearby market were also my thing back then. I loved wearing it like a bejeweled crown and it completed my princess look.

I would like to give credit to the many *Betamax* tapes (kids, feel free to Google this ancient artifact that has changed the lives of many children, including mine, in the 90s) that featured Madonna, and other Disney classics such as Cinderella, Snow White, Sleeping Beauty, and Pinocchio, that my dad would bring us whenever he would come home from Saudi. The movies have greatly inspired and influenced me as much as they have made my childhood a lot more bearable.

Being the youngest, I would often be left alone at home when my older siblings went to school and my mom to the market, or someplace where she could earn a living for the day. With nothing better to do, I would turn on the television and Betamax player, and feed it with whatever tape I desired to watch that day. Sometimes I would spend my afternoon with Madonna, the Seven Dwarves, or with Mr Geppetto tinkering with stuff. On other days, I'd share it with Sleeping Beauty who would eventually influence me to take an afternoon nap.

Because Disney characters had been my constant babysitter, I became fascinated with their world. So much so, that their world had eventually become my diversion when mine would become a little too much to handle for the seven-year-old me.

I would find myself sometimes escaping to their magical world, through my vivid imagination, shortly after surviving my parents' heated argument of the day. This technique has also served as one of my childhood security blankets, apart from my diary entries addressed to God. It has helped me temporarily block off all the taunts and bullying I would get from some kids around me. It gave me comfort and an assurance that everything will be all right in the end. Simply put, it helped me survive an exhausting day.

Allow me to walk you through my memories so you'd better understand what I am talking about. Let's rewind the Betamax tapes of my childhood, shall we?

There was one time when I was clinging on to my mom's leg, bawling, and begging her not to leave our house. I found out that that morning, my dad had been shouting at my mom from our living room to their bedroom where she had slumped, crying. I'd forgotten what exactly they were arguing about. I just clearly remembered how my dad had forcefully driven my mom out of our house while sternly warning us not to go with her.

I also remembered how I shifted from my mom's legs on to my dad's. And how I tightly hugged his hairy legs while on my knees, pleading him to stop shouting. I really wanted him to stop moving toward my mom while angrily shouting so I transferred all my weight and energy from my knees and on to his feet as if it did anything significant. But, I still did it anyway. His irritated screams were so loud that it moved our neighbours to poke their heads out of their house's windows to check what the commotion was in our home.

There was also one weird day when I was sitting on a bench outside our house and my mom sat beside me. A few minutes later, I saw her take out a full pack of paracetamol and she tried to consume everything in one go. I was only about seven years old at this time but I absolutely knew what she was trying to do. She was obviously trying to hurt herself. I was sobbing like crazy. It was an exhausting cryfest for the both of us, to say the least. I kept crying even when I had no more tears to shed. I mean, hello, my mom was trying to hurt herself in front of me. How do you think I should have reacted? I kept telling her to go to the doctor and have herself checked before her condition gets worse. She shrugged me off and told me to just let her be. But I couldn't. How could I? She was my mom!

It was so messed up. She even came to a point where she was already saying her last wishes. Confused yet concerned, because in my head she had just drank a handful of medicine, I replied: 'Mommy, guide *mo pa rin ako kahit nasa* heaven *ka na ha?* (Mommy, please guide me even if you're already in heaven okay?) I meant every word in between sobs. We both were such drama queens at that time. So filled with emotions (I was mostly confused, to be honest) that I felt like my snot had become too shy to come out of my flared nostrils because my mom and I were having an intense moment.

It was so intense that all I could muster was to look up at the sky and think about what was happening in my life. Looking back, it sure would've been nice if Diana Ross's song 'It's My Turn' played in the background and a director would come out of nowhere, and yell 'CUT!' in the next few seconds. None of it happened, of course.

That step to hurt herself was the first of many. And with every attempt, my mom made sure that I was present to see every scene unfolding. I don't know what my mom's deal was but I guess she, too, was so hurt that she wanted to share the painful moment with someone. And the lucky winner was me.

That was my mom's life whenever my dad was home. It had always been a *teleserye-* (soap opera) worthy moment. He and my mom loooooved making a scene. Sometimes gut-wrenching, most of the time humiliating, and nothing close to romantic. And, because I was the youngest, and not too busy with school yet, I became witness to it all.

I recall one 'episode' when, after my parents fought, my mom stormed out of the house and went to the nearby beach. But for my mom to reach the beach, she had to cross a river during low tide. She had to do it quickly because the river rose fast and the current, was stronger. So since it was still low tide, she was able to go even farther on the beach and stayed there, maybe to prove a point or to spite my dad, even when the water had started to rise.

Seeing the water rise, it was my dad's cue to order me to go to where my mom was, and bring her home safely. All of this, while he watched what was happening to my mom, seated comfortably on a chair in our home. Great!

Imagine a petite, adolescent Neri, clueless about the issues that had been going on in her family, obediently crossing the river and walking to the far end of the beach while the tides were rapidly rising at dusk. What a sight, right? I didn't want to do it but I had no choice. I was afraid of being punished and smacked by my dad so I went to get my mom despite the rising tide.

At first, my mom didn't budge. She shooed me off because she was determined to drown her sorrows out; literally. But, I was not. So I convinced her to come back home with me one last time. I was crying my eyes out trying to convince her to move. Had it not been for the fast-rising water, I kid you not, she wouldn't have come with me. With my pruney legs, drenched clothes, and puffy eyes, I brought my mom safely to my dad's arms. I thought they'd eventually kiss and make up but it never happened. They just continued their argument without even asking me if I, their exhausted child, was okay.

The last time I remember my mom was this intense about the desire to hurt herself was when I saw her in her room with a blunt knife in her hand and she was trying to stab her thighs. I tried to stop her but I was too afraid to grab the large knife from her hands so I started crying instead. It was traumatic.

Shortly after, I saw her going up the nearby mountain (walking distance from our house). I had just come from the restroom when I saw her hike up the high mountain in frustrated strides. Knowing all too well that she just wanted to grab my dad's attention, I followed her up to the summit where she said she wanted to hurt herself. So imagine my fear and exhaustion when I found her standing near the edge of the summit. I honestly didn't know what was running in her head at that time but I clearly remember what was in mine.

It was filled with prayers and pleas to God. I kept telling Him to save my mom, to save us, and to help us. Days passed and my parents' arguments sadly continued. It went on until it was time for my dad to go back again to Saudi for work.

Now, please know that I told you all these stories not to paint my parents in a bad light but to illustrate what my life was like. So you can understand better why I preferred to live in a place that exists only in my head and one that only I could access.

To be in this space proved helpful. Whenever my home would become chaotic, I would eventually travel to my imaginary world and snap back to reality when I felt it was safe to go back, one instance was when I experienced unnecessary hate and bullying in school.

Although I had a few friends at school, there were other kids who went out of their way to be mean to me for some reason. There were those who pushed me off a swing I was trying to enjoy just because some kids felt I wasn't worthy of using it because of my social status. There were also others who would pinch me and those who would intentionally make booby traps to hurt me. But, for some unexplainable reason (must be God's grace!) instead of retaliating, I was able to simply ignore the bullying, walk away, and seek refuge in the little sparkly world in my head even if I was hurt and bleeding.

As much as this technique had given me much relief, it has also given other kids my age something to hate me more for. There was no escaping the harsh realities from all sides of my life.

I was living my best one in my imaginary kingdom. But I'd find out later that my tendency to keep to myself and way of dealing with things didn't sit well with some of the kids in school. Instead of being accepted for my quirks, I was even more alienated because of it. Though, again, I had friends who would defend me against the bullies back then (Hi, Lea!) but the other kids were just really mean because of how non-confrontational I was.

I found myself scribbling in my diary and bombarding God with one too many questions about everything that has happened in my life. Why didn't you just give me a better life, God? How long will this pain last?

And in true God fashion, He didn't answer me the way humans would. I would probably be scared if a Morgan Freeman-like voice popped out of nowhere and answered me in the middle of my diary entry writing. That or I would think I have gone crazy.

But also, in true God fashion, He eventually answered me the best way He could through the many people who have made me see and feel what it was like to have hope; to have something to hold on to and look forward to when there seems nothing but darkness.

Combined with my faith in God and the kindness of the adults I have met along the way, I continued to ignore the taunts. I boldly refused to accept the names they were calling me because I believed I was neither an oddball nor delusional. I was God's princess. And in my mind, I continued to have a happy life with my loving family.

I did not entertain the reality that I was a poor kid unworthy of anything good in this world because God has put it in my heart that I am His child. I truly believed that my unfortunate situation then won't be the same situation I'll be in forever. I didn't know what to call it then but my constant conversations with God, through my diary, have helped me develop the habit of hoping for a better future.

Now that I am older, I no longer escape to an imaginary world for comfort but I find it in the fact that I have God. Shit's still going to happen but I am confident that even if it does, God will be with me and help me until the end. He is the provider of my hope.

He has never failed me then, He will never fail me now.

WAIS TIP #16: BE GENEROUS WITH SHARING HOPE. IT'S FREE

I didn't get along with the kids my age for reasons narrated in the previous pages. But you know who I became friends with? The moms in my neighbourhood. SURPRISE!

Perhaps I was drawn to them because I had been longing for a more nurturing and caring mother all these years. And I was able to experience with them the bonding that I never got to experience with my mother. Whenever I was given a chance, I would strike up a conversation with them—be it along the highway on my way home from gathering slops or in their sari-sari store while trying to sweet-talk my way into getting a bottle of soda and *pan de coco* (coconut-filled bread) on credit.

During those brief encounters, we would casually exchange pleasantries. I would ask them how they were and they would receive my occasional yet special Neri compliment.

Their presence and the way they interacted with me somehow gave me a bit of hope every time we would meet. Now, if you are wondering how it is to share hope with someone, here are some of the things that I do that somehow make a huge difference:

1. **LISTEN INTENTLY**

   Resist the urge to listen to respond. Allow other people to talk and talk until they run out of things to say. Let them tell their story. Sometimes, you can try to ask a follow-up question in the end just to make them feel listened to. If this simple gesture made me feel important as a child when other grown-ups took their time to hear what I had to say, imagine how adults would feel.

2. **ACKNOWLEDGE AND APPRECIATE**

   One thing I noticed about what some of our neighbours did when I was younger was—they appreciated and acknowledged what I had made, even if they weren't interested in whatever stuff I was trying to sell them. They seldom told me I was too young to be doing it. If they weren't interested, they would just acknowledge what I was trying to do and compliment how fresh my vegetables were or how my perseverance was admirable for a young girl like me. It inspired me to try again the next day and looked forward to the day when I'd make a huge sale.

3. **DO NOT INVALIDATE A PROBLEM**

    In all fairness to my mom, despite her hitting me often—because that was all she knew when it comes to expressing her feelings whenever she would be irritated by me asking one too many questions or being rowdy as a child—she has never invalidated any of my concerns. She never once told me that I have no right to cry just because I was feeling sad. Or I shouldn't be hurt when bullied because other kids were bullied worse than I was. Instead, she helped me find solutions in her tough-love way, like cooking for me or bringing home yummy treats. Somehow, this simple gesture of hers contributed to my being hopeful growing up.

4. **OFFER SUPPORT**

    The mom-friends who owned sari-sari stores were heaven-sent. I knew we were all trying to make our way in the world so I realized that them being extra forgiving about me having to buy food and other stuff from their stores OFTEN ON CREDIT might be one of their ways of showing support to the little Neri who was also trying to survive. If it wasn't an act of support, I would still thank them for not driving me away or taking it against me. Because of the consideration they have shown and given me, I didn't give up on dreaming that I will soon become successful after finding my own ways. One day, I will come back to visit our town and pay them back. Well, my mom eventually paid most of them before I could but you get the idea.

Hope is free. If we could be anything in this world, let us strive to become each other's light.

Chapter 7

Courage

I will not trade my difficult childhood for anything else in this world. Even if you bribe me with a whole island or a day with Madonna (hmm hold on, let me reconsider … JUST KIDDING!), I will not rearrange or take out anything from my past. Even the most painful moments.

Because for every 'NO', 'STOP', 'NONE', or 'IT CAN'T BE DONE', it drove me closer to becoming the courageous person that I believe I am today and having the kind of life that I have now. You see, for every obstacle I would encounter, I would often be left with two choices: 'GIVE UP' or 'GO'. I would always pick the latter. I remember I would only give up when I felt like I was at a dead-end, my cause wasn't worth it, or I was too sleepy to push through. What can you do, I was a growing child. I needed my naps!

I couldn't remember how exactly I became this courageous person, but I do know that it came along with the hope for a better future. This might be the reason why I had the guts to join a beauty pageant or try out to become a television host even when I barely knew anything about the kind of work I was trying to get into.

Or perhaps, having a courageous heart was one of God's answers to my many 'letters' to Him through my diary. He might have His reasons why He allowed pain, sadness, taunts, discrimination, and all the negativity to happen to me when I was younger. So that when I grew up, I would be someone who would be strong and capable enough to fulfil His plans for my family and for the generations that will come after me.

Maybe it was also included in God's plans that I live to experience all the challenges so I can have something to share with you in this chapter of the book. Come to think of it, if there were no challenges and their corresponding fruits, there wouldn't even be a book. Crazy and exciting isn't it? I guess everything worked out well in the end!

I won't keep you waiting. Let's kick fear in the butt!

WAIS TIP #17: SET A GOAL. WHENEVER YOU FEEL SCARED, GO BACK TO IT AND REMEMBER WHY YOU STARTED AND WHO YOU ARE DOING IT FOR

It's easy for us to get derailed. With the many distractions left, right, and centre, especially in this digital age, discouragement is just a click or a swipe away. Thank God that, when I was growing up, the internet and all these tech gadgets weren't available yet. Had there been Facebook, Instagram, or TikTok when I was still so naive, they sure would have crushed me and my dreams.

If you start feeling the discouragement slowly creeping in while you're in the middle of, let's say, a passion project and you start to think that what you're doing is pointless. Or your idea isn't even that unique. Or worse, you are starting to feel afraid of what other people might say about your passion project! What do you do???

Dig deep into your memory, go back to your notes, and remember why you are doing what you are doing. Doing this will not only get you back on track but it will give you that much-needed boost of courage and confidence to push through.

Do you recall my beauty pageant story that gave birth to an opportunity for me to become a regional television host? My only goal then was to make money. For a child who grew up in poverty, making money was enough motivation for me to suck it up and face my fears.

I will not lie to you and say I had it all under control during that time. Of course not! There were times, during the actual pageant, when I would be tempted to walk away and just go home because I was too scared to mess up on stage. I also wasn't planning on pursuing the hosting stint because I knew nothing about it. I was hesitant because

I was afraid I might mess up in front of hundreds and thousands of viewers. But I needed and wanted to make money for me and my family. At the time, it was enough reason for me to soldier on.

I am well aware that we are all coming from different backgrounds and my situation might be entirely different from yours. Our definitions of scary will surely be different, too. So I would just like to let you know that if and when the scary situation gets the best of you, pause for a moment, take a deep breath, and remember your anchor.

It can be God, your children, your partner, your parents, your dog, your dream of making it in Hollywood, anything, and anyone! Think of it and do your best to focus on it.

WAIS TIP #18: FIGHT FEAR WITH KNOWLEDGE

This is one of my favourites, if not my favourite, fear-busting technique that I have proven to be effective over the years. I have realized that most of the things that scare me are the ones that I know nothing of or I practically have less idea about.

I was hesitant to join the beauty pageant because I haven't had any similar experience before it. I didn't want to go back to the TV station for the next show because I didn't know a thing about TV hosting. I used to be quite scared of public speaking. I would get clammy hands and I would stutter. But because I wanted to see if I could do it, I studied well and even practised with Chito so he could correct my pronunciation. I could have stopped at the first two business franchises because I lacked business know-how. But, I wanted to pursue entrepreneurship so I enrolled in business courses and sought guidance from established entrepreneurs to make sure that my next business ventures are successful.

Long story short, I was not afraid any more because I have studied my enemies (aka the things that intimidate and scare me) so well. Now I can host events or talk on online shows for brands with ease and manage businesses like I have been doing them my whole life!

What I didn't know didn't hurt me but it sure induced a lot of unnecessary fear! What did I do? I studied everything there was to know about the industry or situation I was planning to get into. Doing this helped me assess the situation and plan my next move. It also allowed me to easily manage everything because I am already familiar with it.

I always tell people who ask me for life advice that nothing in this life is ever easy. Fear is and will always be a part of our lives because we are mere humans. But, it is up to us if we'll fight it or succumb to it. Either way, there is going to be a consequence. We just have to choose the one that will propel us forward if our goal is to succeed and to make the most out of our life.

Scared of travelling alone? Research about the country or city you want to go to. Familiarize yourself with the place's customs and traditions so you also don't get in trouble.

Nervous and a bit scared about your job interview? You can easily search for information about the company before your interview day or ask about the company culture before the interview ends. This way, you will have extra information in your arsenal that you can always go back to. These are just some examples but I know you know what I mean.

WAIS TIP #19: TRAIN YOUR MIND TO BECOME A WARRIOR

Our mind, just like our body, is capable of a lot of things when trained properly. Looking back, I thank God that I was subjected to difficult situations. Because my mind, even when I was a child, had been constantly trained to withstand the challenges that I will be facing later in the life. And when I became one, I continued with the training until this very day.

No, I didn't enroll my brain in an American Ninja Warrior camp or subject it to Takeshi's Castle (ooops, another Google-able 90s gem!) obstacle course. Nothing like that. I guess it was more of a daily mental exercise until the mindset became second nature to me.

Allow me to share with you some of the pep talks that have helped my mind become stronger each day. And remember, just like everything else in this book, there's no need for you to do all or religiously follow every single piece of advice. Just take what you need and use it the best way you can! You can even write on a sticky note the ones that resonate with you the most, and post them on your bathroom mirror or your work area.

1. Other people's opinions do not matter unless they contribute to my progress.
2. The more I become familiar with my obstacle, the easier I conquer it.
3. It's okay if I feel scared right now. This is just temporary. I will get through this and I will not let this stop me.
4. I won't know the answer if I don't ask. I won't know the outcome if I don't try.
5. You have dreams, you have ambitions **Neri** (you can change this to your name). And you will not achieve them if you do not have the courage to take the leap.
6. The strength that you have right now is all you need. God will sustain you!
7. If I don't do it, who will? If I don't do it now, then when?
8. If other people can do it, I can do it too!
9. I don't want to live a life filled with 'WHAT Ifs'.

Just a friendly reminder my fellow Wais Na Misis. Being Wais also means that we are aware that people are built differently. So, when trying to encourage another person, be it a friend, a colleague, or a family member, keep in mind that that person might be coming from a place of fear or trauma that we have no idea of, so tread lightly. Be gentle with your words.

WAIS TIP #20: WHEN SOMEONE IS AFRAID, TRY TO BE WITH THEM UNTIL THEY ARE NOT

We can pep talk people as much as we want. We can post encouraging messages on our friends' walls anytime we wish. But sometimes, there's something a bit more comforting when an actual person is beside you; helping you conquer the challenge, and sharing the experience with you.

I have always been afraid of crossing streets, most especially highways since I was a child. Why wouldn't I be when I was THISCLOSE to being swiped by a speeding bus one afternoon? So, more than being left alone or having to talk to my neighbours, I dreaded crossing the highway. When I attempted to, I was just not sure if some of my dear neighbours or random passers-by had walked me safely to the other side and back, but I knew I was able to survive that obstacle because there were people who were with me as I crossed the highway.

Of course, there are rare days when my mom would be with me. It was mainly because I probably begged her if I could go with her to wherever she was going so I could have an adult with me to cross the streets and highways. She would often be hesitant but nevertheless I'm still thankful.

When my children call for me in the middle of the night, I gather whatever ounce of strength I am able to regenerate so I can open my eyes, rise from my sleep, and check up on them. Their reasons may be as simple as wanting to be clingy or it might be as alarming as them having nightmares. Whatever their reason may have been, my being there is a clear message that they will always have someone whom they can call whenever they feel scared. And that they shouldn't be afraid of being afraid because it's normal.

Being aware and admitting that you are afraid is the first step to conquering it. There's nothing shameful about it.

Later on, I was able to explain to my kids that the person whom they count on for help can be anyone from our family. Or that can be God, my number one rescuer then and now. I also shared with them my experiences of when I would be so scared of crossing the highway but no grown-up would be present to hold my hand or walk me through. So I called on God and prayed to cross the highway safely because I had pigs to feed and I needed to get my slop-gathering work done. Sometimes, I would even pray aloud and say. 'God, *tulungan N'yo po akong makatawid. Natatakot po ako sa mga bus pero kailangan ko na po tumawid.* Please please please!' (God, help me cross the highway. I'm scared of the buses but I badly need to cross now.)

Of course, God didn't appear out of thin air and escort me to the other side of the highway. That would have been a creepy experience for a child. But, I still remembered the unexplainable confidence I'd felt the instant I said that plea. I still cannot clearly describe it until now but the scary thought of being run over by a speeding bus was wiped out of my heart and mind. And the feeling of confidence that I will be able to cross the highway unharmed, took over my tiny ten-year-old body.

WAIS TIP #20: WHEN YOU FEEL SCARED, PRAY

Do you remember the diary I told you about, the one where I write all my worries and dreams and some grateful praises addressing to God? Looking back, writing in the diary has opened my communication lines with God. It eventually helped me create a relationship with Him through our constant conversations. Though He doesn't exactly respond the way we humans do (like talk to us, send us an e-mail or a Viber message, or visit us at home to personally be with us), I still have learned how to be open to Him about almost everything. Because of this, I have developed this kind of confidence that He hears me; that He is someone that I can always run to for whatever reason I may have; and that He always answers the best way He knows how.

I grew up a devoted Catholic and my prayer life and relationship with God were what made me decide to share with you this Wais Tip. I held on to this verse and prayed when I found myself in the middle of my parents' fighting storm; when I would cross the streets and highways; when we would desperately hide from the landlord who was angrily looking for us because we have missed paying our rent for the nth time; when I tried to live on my own in the city; when I faced the scandal and gossips when I was still active in showbusiness; when I had a miscarriage; when my previous businesses failed; when some of my trusted people betrayed me because of money; and when reality sometimes hit me with thoughts and questions if I am being a good mother.

These were some of the scary situations that I was able to eventually face because of prayer and God's grace. Though, please be warned that God's ways aren't our ways so don't be discouraged if you feel like your prayers aren't being answered. Just keep on doing it. Trust that He will answer in His perfect time and ways. And know, too, that if He heard my prayers when I was scared, He will definitely hear yours, too.

WAIS TIP #21: YOU EITHER WIN OR YOU LEARN

This next story is filled with grade school mischief and childhood foolishness that I highly advise you to take every word you read hereafter lightly. I blame it on my carefree youth and my adorable friends.

Here's a story I am not exactly proud of, but it's one that has taught me a valuable lesson that I carry to this day.

I was around twelve years old then when my school in Subic prepared a camping programme exclusively for Girl Scouts. I wanted to join so badly because most of my friends were Girl Scout members and, let's not kid ourselves here, I didn't want to miss out on the fun! My mom didn't allow me because she didn't have enough money to pay for the camping fee which at the time was Php 100. It was so hard for me to believe what she had just said because, at that time, I would see how my mom would squander most of our money and spend it all on gambling. So, I respectfully pleaded but she didn't budge.

Like a dutiful daughter, I told my classmates and friends that I wasn't allowed to go and that we didn't have money for the camping fee.

They must've seen how much I'd wanted to go and, well, they must have also wanted me to be there, so they came up with a feasible but risky plan. They all pooled a portion of their allowances so they could pay for my camping fee. And, oh my goodness, my classmates signed (more of forged perhaps? Haaay kids, don't do this!) the permit and waiver that my mom was supposed to sign so I'd be allowed to join. And when it was all covered, they devised a plan to try and sneak me out of our house after I came home from school.

The plan became too easy since my mom had been out playing *MahJong* and gambling since morning and didn't come home until later that day, so I had the house all to myself. I took the chance to quickly pack my overnight bag and throw in a couple of canned tuna for safety. I also wrote an apology letter on the back of the camping permit to appease my conscience.

My letter read:

Ma,

Sorry po nasa camping ako. Kinuha ako ng mga classmates ko na naawa sa akin. Sila na rin po ang nagbayad ng camping fee. Sorry po pero gusto ko talagang sumama. (Sorry, I went camping. My classmates fetched me because they felt sorry for me. They have also paid for my camping fee. I am sorry but I really wanted to go.)

Bunso

Before I headed out to meet my classmates, I took a deep breath, said a short prayer, and posted the letter on our refrigerator for my mom to read later when she got home.

It was *one* of the most daring, if not the most daring, decisions I've made as an adolescent. It was scary, I must admit, but it was fun too! Looking back I think, that wasn't the best move and I probably shouldn't have done it, but oh well, everything turned out fine in the end.

My friends and I were having a blast at the camp. We were only allowed to cook our own meals using ingredients that the camp organizers had prepared and with the vegetables gathered from the school's vegetable garden. It was school camping, a simulation of what it was like to live in the wilderness. Obviously, pre-cooked food or instant meals weren't allowed, not even eggs. Where in the real wilderness do you think you'll see canned goods and instant noodles popping up like mushrooms? Nowhere. Or do you often see someone bringing a pack of warm home-cooked meals to you in the middle of the night? Yep, no one.

So imagine my surprise when one of my classmates shouted, although softly, *'Nerizza, yung nanay mo and'yan!'* (Nerizza, your mom's there!) pointing to the entrance of the campsite. As soon as the word *'nanay'* reached my ears, I quickly froze inside our tent. Beads of sweat had started to form on my forehead. And, you guessed it, I began praying to God, saying whatever plea I could think of just so my mom wouldn't scold me in front of my classmates. Or worse, slap me hard in the face. Knowing my mom, that was a possibility, too.

It was a warm night but I was shaking like I had been trapped inside the refrigerator for hours. I had been dishonest, I snuck out of our house, I lied, and I now was trapped. My mom was on her way to our area and I had no way out.

Sensing my doom, I went out of our tent and slowly walked toward the direction of my mom. Hundreds of excuses and apologies had been brewing in my head as I inched my way to face my fear that night. I could've just chickened out and stayed inside the tent until she was gone. But, I have realized that I had to face the consequences of my actions and sincerely apologize for my mistakes. That's what God would've wanted me to do, too. Also, if I succumbed to my fear at that time, I'd most probably be scared again and I didn't want that. I didn't want to live in fear for the rest of my life. So, I faced my mom.

I was staring at the ground the entire time I was walking to where my mom was. With my eyes half-closed, I slowly lifted my head while holding my breath in anticipation of the loudest and strongest slap my twelve-year-old face would ever receive.

My mom held out her hand and I flinched, thinking she was about to hit me. But to my surprise, I saw her hand holding what looked like a plastic bag with a whole grilled fish inside. Then she asked me if I'd already eaten. I shook my head shyly and she handed me the grilled fish.

Then she left.

I was still in shock but the smell of the grilled fish made my mouth water. I quickly ran back to our tent to share the good news and the food. Like the rascals that we were, we ate with so much gusto. We even shared the fish with our teacher, who caught us eating something that wasn't cooked at the campsite, just so she wouldn't reprimand us.

It was a pretty intense scenario, one that could compete with *Jumanji*'s or *Mission Impossible*'s most heartstopping scenes. It was also a teachable moment for me. And like what I told you at the beginning of this WAIS TIP, this particularly laughable story was where I have learned one of the most important lessons that I keep in mind till this day: If something is worth doing, TAKE THE RISK.

In my case, the answers were either I was going to get slapped or I'll be gifted with grilled fish. Life's like that. You'll never know if there's even grass on the other side if you don't check and see for yourself. And you'll never know what the answer is if you don't ask.

Take the chance today. Tomorrow's never promised.

Chapter 8

Failure

If there's one thing I can say I am quite good at—it's failing. Now, before you close this book and decide you don't want to continue reading any more because '*Neri's going to be talking about a negative word, and I don't want any of it ...*' please read it further for a short while before you decide.

Since we have just talked about courage in the previous chapter, I have decided to write a full chapter about failing. It's often regarded as a negative word but it produces a lot of positive outcomes. At first, I thought that it was something that I should avoid or be scared of. But it was one of the reasons why I am who I am today. In fact, I also consider it to be one of the key ingredients in achieving whatever purpose or goals I may have had and may still have in my life.

Instead of cursing it or running away from it at first sight, I had made a friend out of failure. I would entertain it, face it, sit beside it, grieve with it, and even share an ice-cold glass of Coke zero or two with it. Now it has warmed up to me and it doesn't hesitate to reveal the gift it has been hiding from me when I was too prideful and stubborn to see.

When failure is convinced that I have already accepted its gift, it quietly leaves. It makes sure I don't see it again until it decides to bring me a new gift. Because failure, unlike an annoying and unwanted guest, doesn't like outstaying its welcome. It leaves at the exact moment it has finally accomplished its mission; the day I learned my lesson.

There is so much wisdom hidden in every failure. I pray to live long enough so I can continuously learn from life and have time to share it with others.

WAIS TIP #22: FAILURE IS AS NORMAL AS SUCCESS

What you read about my businesses and the kind of life that I am living right now are just the products of years of hard work, late-night grind, trial-and-error, and generous servings of failure. Yes, you read that right. FAILURE.

Since it has been given a bad image, often equating to defeat and the lack of whatever it is that's needed to ensure a favourable result, it doesn't get as much limelight and exposure as the word 'success'. Because of this, we would often avoid it like a plague. As much as I would have liked to avoid failure, it hounded me like a puppy during my younger years.

I failed in the show business department. Not that I was incapable of being one but, I wasn't able to fully flourish as one. But, without my failed attempt to make it big in the industry, I wouldn't have had the leverage (budget and reach) to become the business person that I am today.

Pre-pandemic, I have also tried my hand at franchising a milk tea business and putting up a pharmacy. Both had tremendously failed, and I had lost almost a million pesos, or even more! I'd like to attribute the failure to my lack of business know-how at that time. But, because of what happened, it pushed me to sharpen my skills more so it doesn't happen again.

Without it, I wouldn't have known what I did wrong and what needs improvement for further plans and ideas to succeed. I would like to compare failure to yeast. As it is, it may just look like normal seasoning granules. Sometimes, it smells funky too. But, as much as it looks unnecessary, it is a key ingredient in the making of fluffy and tasty bread.

Now these are the things that we don't usually read in the news or see on television because we are so used to reporting or highlighting mostly the results that are positive and inspirational.

Failure can be inspiring, too.

WAIS TIP #23: IT'S OKAY TO BE NUMBER 2, 3, 4, 5, OR 6! (EXCEPT IN ROMANTIC RELATIONSHIPS, OKAY?!)

As much as it pushes me to strive to become better, failure has taught me contentment, too. I was a go-getter as a child and eventually, grew up to become one as well. When I was younger, I used to view success as being the best or having the top number spot. What do I know? It was all just a concept in my head until I subjected myself to numerous competitions such as the regional beauty pageant, the TV hosting stint, and the one that you're probably familiar with: Star Circle Quest.

It was the first of its kind on Philippine television back in 2014, so hundreds and thousands of Filipinos religiously tuned in every night. It was also the show that helped launch some of today's famous celebrities' showbiz careers. With all these people surrounding the show, it indeed was a big deal. And I must admit, the kind of exposure that I have gotten from joining the contest was more than enough to launch me to stardom.

I came in sixth and looking back, it isn't that bad. I may have thought for a time that I had been a failure for not making it to the top but now, observing how my life has turned out, I'm glad I even had the chance of being at the sixth place. I could have gone back home with nothing.

Standing in the sixth place, I have learned that:

1. **There are still more opportunities waiting for me.** Even if I didn't win the grand prize, I was still able to continue my acting career for several years before going full-time as an entrepreneur. I was also offered amazing acting roles and good guesting stints even when I didn't win the top spot.
2. **The sixth place was just a marker.** I did not allow my failure to define me and my skills beyond the confines of the show. I believed that I am more than the ranking and that I am capable of achieving more.
3. **It kept me on my toes.** Being in the sixth place challenged me to become better at my craft. I have developed the mindset that I should continuously be improving and evolving so people will

see me beyond the initial ranking from the show where I came from. Plus, I have realized that it has been keeping me grounded all these years. I had no grand prize to bank on, so I relied on God's grace, on His opportunities, and on the skills that He has given me to make it big in the industry.

4. **Being too focused on becoming the first may have prevented me from enjoying the moment.** Had I become too obsessed with winning the grand prize, I surely wouldn't have enjoyed my journey. I wouldn't have made friends either, that I still keep in touch with till date. I also wouldn't have remembered every bit of the experience and savoured everything that was unfolding in front of me, because my eyes were too focused on being the first.

There are still more learnings that I want to share but I'm going to keep it at four for now. You'll find out more in the next chapters of this book anyway.

As I have said in Wais Tip #21, there is no losing in this life. We either win or we learn. And all the events wherein I thought I have lost, I actually gained a lot of valuable lessons that I know I wouldn't learn from anywhere else.

WAIS TIP #24: A FAILURE WILL REMAIN A FAILURE UNTIL YOU DO SOMETHING ABOUT IT

John Maxwell, an American leadership expert and author, and Denzel Washington, a famous American actor, both have talked about the concept of 'Failing Forward'. The former, through his inspirational books, and the latter, through his commencement speech dedicated to the graduating class of the University of Pennsylvania back in 2011.

They talk of embracing failure and using it as a stepping stone to a better way of life, career path, and personal progress. They have also shared that, for us to be able to truly overcome failure, it is important that we own the situation by acknowledging it and taking concrete steps to learn from what has already happened and putting it to use in order to improve.

As a former actress and now an entrepreneur, of course, I have had my share of downs that I don't often talk or post about. But instead of focusing on what went wrong, let me share with you the steps I took to make my failure work to my advantage.

1. **Don't be afraid to ask for feedback.** This move used to scare the heck out of me. Anxious thoughts would quickly rush to my head. What if they tell me I sucked? What if they say I am not good enough? What if they confirm the negative things that are already in my head about myself? Will I be able to handle all those perceptions?

   It is quite disheartening, to be honest, but I believe that asking for feedback (from a credible and reliable person) is a powerful way of using failure to my advantage. I did this when I was still active in show business and I am still doing this to improve how I run and handle my businesses. I seek feedback from my team, a couple of experts, and other people who may know more about the business than I do. Doing this gives me valuable insights into what went wrong so I can correct and improve my strategies.

2. **Keep an open mind.** Sure, this is easier said than done when we are dealing with a situation that is not something to be proud of. But having this mindset has helped me grow as a person and as an entrepreneur. I used to get a bit defensive whenever I'd fail at something but I realized that having this kind of attitude has prevented me from using the unfavourable circumstance as an opportunity to use for my improvement. Being a Wais Na Misis also means you leave no room for ego in your system.

3. **Try not to take failures personally.** Again, this is something that is easier said than done. That's why I suggested that you simply try. Because taking it personally is a natural and common reaction to faiures, especially if you are like me who pours out your heart, mind, and passion into every project or idea. However, as I matured, I thank God I was able to eventually learn how to separate myself from the failure. It was a part of my growth but it is not and will never be a reflection of my worth as a person and my identity. Given this, when I am in the process of analyzing my previous decisions and strategizing my next moves, I put more focus on the plan and less on my personal shortcomings.

4. **Think of new goals to achieve.** My tough childhood has helped me develop my 'never say die!' attitude. Each time I would encounter a roadblock, my mind would automatically think of a new way around, over, under, and through it. Sometimes, I would crush it so hard that often I would be surprised at myself, for reshaping the intimidating roadblock into a sculpture or a pot that I could sell. Remember, just because your road is blocked doesn't mean you should stop on your first attempt.

WAIS TIP #25: EXPERIENCE THE DARK TO APPRECIATE THE LIGHT

I did not succeed as an actress. Although I did a few projects that I am truly proud of such as *The Legal Wife*, a drama TV series back in 2014 where I played a small but significant role. I still feel as if I never really made it to match the industry's standards. By that, I meant I was not the crowd's favourite, to say the least, because I was the total opposite of the kind of pretty girl the industry usually adores.

Even then, my skin wasn't milky white, I didn't have dainty facial features, and I wore clothes from the thrift store. I mean, hello, what was I to do? I came from a province. I had no idea about the stereotypical pretty city girl look and vibe back in those days. I simply dived in wearing my best. But, as James Ingram would sing, 'My best wasn't good enough' for the industry I was trying to thrive and fit in.

I was laughed at and discriminated against because I was a *probinsyana* (a girl from the province). The taunts and bullying had become so intense that I eventually decided to leave show business, the world that I once thought I'd grow old in, to focus on finishing my studies and pursuing full-time entrepreneurship. It was so messed up that at one point I'd begged my manager to tell our boss to just kill my character in a show. I wanted to get it over with and done with.

Because of my horrifying experiences in show business (I'll be sharing more about it in the next chapters of this book so keep on reading), I have developed a deeper appreciation for the kind of work I have and the people surrounding me right now. It may have its own version of challenges but I know that those are worth enduring.

My only baby photo left—I think I was three years old here, 1986

I used to attend Sagala because my mom forced me, 1990

Senior prom with my friends, 2000

College girl, 2002

When I joined a pageant in Baguio City, 2003

When I joined a talent search, 2004

The pioneers of Neri's Gourmet Tuyo, 2015

My very first Airbnb business: Neri's Cottage, 2015

My very first online business: Very Neri Beddings, 2016

My very supportive husband, 2016

One of the first businesses that I started, 2017

Building Miranda's Rest House, 2017

I started small before I had restaurants: Neri's Bakeshop, 2018

One of Neri's Gourmet Tuyo outlets in SM malls, 2018

Busy in the kitchen of Neri's Cafe, 2019

Live band every week in my cafe, 2019

Neri's Cafe, 2019

Wow! Finished my Harvard Online Business course, 2020

Gardening is my passion, 2020

Harvesting peanuts, 2020

With my mom at my garden, 2020

Juggling motherhood and business, 2021

We have a pizza parlour! Amare La Cucina, 2021

This was three weeks after I gave birth to Cash . . . we opened an
Italian restaurant, Amare Restaurant, 2021

We are now part of Jaytee's, 2022

Cash's baptism, 2022

Family picture, 2022

Finally, I have my college diploma! 2022

Opening of my salon: ExtraordiNeri, 2022

Unli Samgyupsal at our Jeju Samgyupsal Resto in Cebu, 2022

Recent family picture, 2023

With the grandmothers, 2023

Chapter 9

Faith

How do I even begin this chapter? How is it any different from hope? Can we have hope without faith or vice versa? How does one develop faith? These questions and thoughts might take up the whole chapter if I try to expound on them. I probably have little to no knowledge about the technicalities of each word and might mess it up while trying to help you understand. So, let me just share with you my journey and my life with the one who has never left my side, no matter how stubborn I'd sometimes get, all these years—my God.

I came to know Him when I was around six or seven years old. I have forgotten how exactly but I knew of His existence even then, though I haven't seen Him in the flesh (has anyone?!). I grew up a devoted Catholic. I would go to church every Sunday and actively participate in Mass. My grandmother would also make me attend church activities such as processions and other events that required me to wear a matching set of white dress, white shoes with white stockings. I enjoyed participating in those kinds of activities so much because I loved dressing up and I was passionate about participating in all kinds of church activities, so much so that I didn't mind if the lacey dress made my whole body itch the entire time I was wearing it. I kept scratching my legs and arms, but I didn't care because I was having a blast!

I also thought I would eventually become a nun as I was almost always in church serving. I would always volunteer to participate in Holy Week activities at school whenever given the chance. In fact, I went to school early to attend the morning mass, and my siblings would tease and laugh at me because of it. They'd jokingly ask if I owned the school because I would be the first student to enter and the last one to leave because of my commitment to the activities.

As a child, I used to fear God the way I would fear my parents because I was afraid I would get punished if I didn't act or behave well. But all these changed when I developed a relationship with Him through the diary entries that were addressed to Him. When the usual entries of others start with *Dear Diary,* mine mentioned *Dear God.* I figured that the latter had a nicer ring to it and felt more personal. It was as if the God I was addressing the letters to might respond any moment.

Written in my diary were my happiest highs and deepest lows. I know I never wrote anything that was close to boring or normal because I just didn't feel like it.

Instead, I love remembering those moments that have contributed to my core memories; those that have taught me important lessons that I still sometimes follow to this day. I was also fond of updating God about the events that have put a smile on my face and the ones that have made me cry. Sometimes, I'd tell Him the ones that have angered me so much that I almost tore the pages because I was intensely writing every word. Whatever happened that day, I knew that I wanted and needed to let God know about it. After all, even if I had a family, I had no one to share my thoughts and feelings with, at any time I wished.

WAIS TIP #26: I ALWAYS REMEMBER THAT PEOPLE MAY NOT ALWAYS BE THERE FOR ME, BUT GOD WILL

One of the reasons why I was fond of writing in my diary and addressing every entry to God, was I was often left alone at home. My dad worked abroad; my mom was either out trying to sell all sorts of stuff or gambling with our neighbours; and my older siblings were usually in school.

As much as I would've loved to create a mother-daughter bond with my mom, sadly, she wasn't the kind of mother who would go out of her way to spend time with me or tuck me to bed at night. She wasn't exactly the warm, motherly kind, but always remained a nice person.

Before, I used to ask God why He gave me Miss Minchin for a mother. (For reference, Miss Minchin was a character in the famous 90s Japanese animated series called *Princess Sara*, which was based on the book *A Little Princess* by Frances Hodgson Burnett. Miss Minchin was the headmistress of the boarding school where Sara Crewe went and was the antagonist of the series as she was known to mistreat Sara during her stay. The character also gained popularity among Filipino kids in the 90s because of it. And later on, she became a pop culture reference for women who are often grumpy, with antagonistic tough love tendencies.) Now, again, this is not to badmouth my mother or paint her in a bad light. I love her and now that I have matured, I have come to realize that she was just shaped differently by her past experiences. I am simply sharing with you why I wasn't able to open up to her when I was younger and Miss Minchin was the closest character I can think of when I thought of describing her.

Anyway, my mother was a disciplinarian. She was so strict that even my high school classmates in Baguio were scared of visiting our home because of her. I had many attempts to come close to her when I was younger, but I was unsuccessful. She was just too closed off.

Fortunately, I had Rani and Kathleen, my two dearest friends who I treasure a lot and still stay in touch with. But when I couldn't be with them, especially Rani, because my mom didn't allow me to leave the house, it was me and my diary at the end of the day.

I guess it had to be that way because, through my diary moments, I was able to form a solid relationship with God without realizing it. Just like when you constantly talk to a person, you eventually develop a certain kind of closeness in the process. That was what happened between me and God. He became my go-to person for every emotion that I've felt and for every core memory that I've experienced. Even when I had the most difficult questions, I would go talk to Him through my diary because I knew He would answer me in the best way He knew.

We share a deeply personal relationship that even now I find difficult to describe or quantify. All I know is that the kind of faith I had in God when I was younger and the one that I now have—both have given me so much comfort and company during my difficult days.

WAIS TIP #27: HAVING FAITH IN GOD HAS TAUGHT ME HOW TO FULLY SURRENDER

There are things in this life that are out of our hands. No matter how much we want to foresee or control the outcomes, our human capabilities can only do so much—yes, even if you are a genius or an extremely talented one at that.

The moment I understood that having faith in God—in someone greater than myself or even my parents—I was able to finally acknowledge that there really were some things that were beyond my control. I have learned to surrender because of that. Not the hopeless kind of surrender but a trusting one.

When the kids bullied me, I knew that I wouldn't be able to do something about it on my own. Retaliating was not an option. Not because I was scared of confrontation but because I was never a supporter of violence. I have had enough of it at home. What I did was I jumped right into my make-believe world in my head, focused on the happy things in it, and offered my bullies to God. I was confident that He would help me deal with the bullies His way, not mine.

In the past, when gossip, judgment, and other hurtful accusations were thrown at me, I almost immediately surrendered them to God. My faith has allowed me to escalate the matters to someone who could indeed do something about the situation because I knew deep in my heart that it will be resolved His way. And His ways are always better than whatever scheme I can think of in my limited human mind.

I grew up carrying this habit of total surrender whenever I dealt with tough situations. Because of this, I seldom waste my precious time and energy dealing with people and situations that would not add any value to my life. When faced with a dead-end, I get on my knees, put my palms up, and offer the obstacle to God. Surrendering may mean defeat to some but for me, I win each time I do it. In fact, it has allowed me to live my best life. I was able to release the weight of my worries, pains, and anxieties to a being greater than myself.

WAIS TIP #28: I KEEP A CHILDLIKE FAITH

Whenever my mom would tell me I couldn't join a school activity because we didn't have money, I wouldn't doubt her words. When my dad told me to fetch my mom in the middle of a fast-rising river, I obeyed his command without questioning why he would not do the fetching himself and send me instead. When I finished elementary, I never questioned why we didn't eat at the famous restaurant in Olongapo where we would usually go and celebrate only special occasions.

I was more than willing to accept things as they were without the need for any logical explanation from either of my parents. In my head and my heart, I had this unexplainable trust that they wouldn't lie to me even if I kind of knew they would. And if they did, I was pretty sure that they had their reasons.

I'd have to thank God for developing this kind of faith in me that I carry to this day. Although now, I know better than to fully trust people blindly and foolishly. Having a childlike faith in God gives me comfort in times of distress. It also helps me understand that though we live in a broken world, there is still so much goodness left for us in it. I may not see it right away, but I trust God, just as I have trusted Him when I was younger, that He will not deprive me and you of all the good things in this lifetime because we are His children. It may sound idealistic for now but once you get into a deeper relationship with Him, as I did, you will fully know what I am talking about.

Keeping a childlike faith also reminds me that there is nothing too small or too big in this world that God cannot provide if you ask according to His will.

WAIS TIP #29: TRUST THAT OUR PRAYERS WILL BE ANSWERED IN GOD'S TIME

In the middle of random conversations or heart-to-heart talks with Chito, I would often find myself wondering why God allowed me to experience the kind of childhood I had. Why, of all people, my mother became my mother; why I was born in a silong when I could have been delivered in a state-of-the-art operating room and welcomed in an air-conditioned suite of one of the Philippines' top hospitals; and why I was given these kinds of problems.

My husband would gently remind me: *'Yung mga challenges na nangyari sa'yo, madalas hindi mo pa talaga maiintindihan kung bakit binigay sa'yo ang mga 'yan. Pero magtiwala ka na masasagot din kung bakit binigay sa'yo ni Lord ang mga problemang ganyan in His time.* Trust the process. *Lahat may rason kahit minsan pakiramdam natin unfair. Pero, hindi din naman fair ang buhay talaga* so it's up to us *kung paano natin 'to ihahandle habang inaantay natin yung sagot sa mga tanong at prayers.'* (Oftentimes, you won't really understand why the challenges were given to you. But trust that your questions, as to why the Lord gave you those kinds of problems, will be answered in His time. Trust the process. Everything happens for a reason even when we feel like it's unfair sometimes. But then again, life isn't fair so it's really up to us how we will handle our problems while waiting for the answers to our questions and prayers.)

I thank God for my childlike faith for it allows me to be expectant, grateful, and hopeful while patiently waiting for His answers. Until then, I will continue to improve myself, serve my family, and enjoy the life that God gave me the grace to live.

Chapter 10

Gratitude

As soon as I open my eyes in the morning, I take a deep breath and try my hardest to think of the things that I am thankful for as I exhale. Believe me when I say I wasn't like this many years ago. I used to reach for my phone and scroll through Google and my social media pages the moment I opened my eyes. It gave me nothing but a list of unnecessary things to be anxious about. Whatever I fed my mind in the mornings, I unconsciously carry it throughout my day. Imagine the kind of burden I had subjected myself to when I could've simply lived a worry-free day. Whatever negativity I had absorbed would reflect in my mood and I didn't like it, so I decided to activate the attitude of gratitude.

I came from a world where luxury was out of reach and the bare necessities were sometimes hard to get, too. There were days when my mom would just have 20 pesos in her cashbox and her resourcefulness would be the only way we could eat.

I was already in third year of high school when I first set foot in a McDonald's in Manila where I got to taste their famous burger for the first time. If it weren't for my relatives who treated me to a meal, I wouldn't have been able to afford one and experience what children as young as two years old would normally experience now. Growing up, while the kids my age would think of what their next snack could be or what game they would play as soon as they woke up from their afternoon nap, my mind would try to think of ways to earn and survive. That was how my mind was greatly affected and reshaped by poverty.

These are just some of the things that, looking back, used to break my young heart. I remember I would even make a special diary entry about all these heartaches and disappointments. But over time, I have seen how the same reasons that made me sad have become the ones that keep my heart in a grateful disposition all these years. Had these not happened, I probably won't be as appreciative of what I have in my life right now. I might be in a state of discontent, who knows? What's more important for me now is that I will always have those experiences to look back to and re-learn from.

WAIS TIP #30: BEING GRATEFUL HELPS IMPROVE OVERALL HEALTH

I used to think that gratitude is just thanking God for whatever blessings I have in my life. That was it. I didn't realize that one simple act can also help my physical, mental, and spiritual health which has allowed me to live a more fulfilling life.

Below are some of the significant changes that I've observed in my life when I consciously became grateful, especially on sad and tough days. Gratitude has helped me see the world in a completely different perspective, eventually opening my eyes to a better world that I pray, one day, you get to experience too!

1. **I have formed better relationships.** Because I was vocal about being thankful for the connections and relationships that I have built, the people around me have started to do it as well. This simple act has also jumpstarted positive communication and increased empathy and compassion within my family and business community. The teamwork and harmony I experience is priceless.
2. **My stress level has been low.** Being grateful has taught me a lot about contentment. I can appreciate people more because I do not expect a whole lot from them based on my standards alone. Because of this, I have often found myself smiling than complaining and winning instead of whining.
3. **I can easily think of solutions.** With the attitude of gratitude, I have learned how to shift my focus to the possibilities of the situations rather than pour my energy into what went wrong or what was lacking. I have become mentally agile, I realized, as this

helps make more space in my head to think of even more creative ways to solve a problem.

4. **I do not take anything for granted.** Most of what I was enjoying when I was a penniless young girl were mere hopes, dreams, and prayers. Because I am grateful for the houses I own now (back then we used to just rent small ones, and most of the time, we couldn't even pay rent on time!), I make sure to take care and make the most of it while I still can. Because despite my mom's tough love, I am thankful she still strived so hard to provide for us so we can have a better life. Now that I am capable of earning, I make sure to provide everything for her in return. I vowed to take care of her and keep the remaining days of her life joyful and stress-free.

5. **I take care of myself more.** I could've been dead; I could've been somewhere other than my home. I could have even lived another life that's less favourable than what I have right now. Knowing all of this, pushes me to value myself even more. I exercise, I eat healthy, I pamper myself well, and I take ample rest whenever I can because I am simply grateful I am where God has placed me at this very moment.

WAIS TIP #31: GRATITUDE IS A CONSCIOUS DECISION

We aren't hardwired to always see the good in every situation. As flawed humans, sometimes our natural tendencies are to find fault and crave the negative. Of course, I will not lie to you and tell you that being grateful comes easy for me. Sometimes, it does when I think of my life back in Subic and Baguio. But, there are ugly days when it would be a task for me to even think of being grateful, let alone actually be one.

Sadness, anger, and other negative emotions prevent me from easily praising God and thanking Him for all His blessings. When this happens, I always remember that gratitude takes practice, too. I consciously do it until it becomes second nature to me.

To get into the habit, I would follow the following techniques that I have learned from the many books and articles I have read. Now remember, as with any other list in this book, feel free to customize it.

No need to follow everything to the dot. Just choose the ones that apply to your situation and make the most out of it. Don't forget to have fun!

1. **INHALE DEEPLY, EXHALE SLOWLY.** Each morning, as soon as I open my eyes I stare at the ceiling or Cash's chubby cheeks and I breathe slowly. This reminds me of the precious gift of being able to live another day. Whenever I feel stressed, I do this breathing technique to remind myself to go easy on myself and try to focus on the good that is in front of me today.

2. **MAKE A GRATITUDE LIST.** Remember how I love writing all my ideas and thoughts in my designated notebooks during my early morning ME Time? Those thoughts include the list of things that I am thankful for and I write it in my DREAM notebook. On days when I feel defeated and get immensely discouraged to push through a project or a decision, I just read through my gratitude and dream lists to regain my focus.

   Now, when you are writing your own, try not to be pressured to put grand or impressive things on your gratitude list. It can be as simple as being thankful for your dog or your husband for taking care of your kids so you can have an extended nap time. If you are having a hard time thinking of anything because you might be in a bad mood, try asking yourself 'What made me laugh so hard today?' or 'What exciting thing or events am I looking forward to tomorrow or next week?' Just remember to keep it simple and always keep it real.

3. **LIVE ONE DAY AT A TIME.** I used to be impatient with almost everything because I either wanted to have things done now or I looked too far ahead into the future that I had forgotten how to appreciate all the good things surrounding then. When I feel discontent and in a hurry, I often tell myself, I only have today. I pause for a moment and I try to take in everything that is happening around me; consciously taking note of all the beautiful gifts I should be thankful for. Doing this has helped me shift my focus from worrying about my future to enjoying what today has to offer. This mindset has brought me a newfound joy in life.

4. **KNOW THAT EVERYTHING IS TEMPORARY.** In relation to living one day at a time is the awareness that all things in this world do not last forever. Cars depreciate, fashion becomes outdated, babies grow old, plants wilt, and food expires. This mindset helps me prioritize what truly matters in my life. Since I am now aware that everyone and everything can be taken away from me at any moment, I do my best to enjoy them the best way I can today. Sometimes when I feel a bit ungrateful, I'd challenge myself and ask: 'If I don't feel grateful for what I already have, what makes me think I'd be happy if I had more?'

5. **BE EXPRESSIVE ABOUT IT.** I know this part may not apply to everyone and that's okay. But for those who are comfortable with showing people and telling them what you are thankful for, by all means, do it. Grab the opportunity! Take this as a sign that it's time to let your parents know how thankful you are to them for raising you. Thank your colleagues for having your back at your workplace meeting. If you have extra budget to spare, you can treat your spouse to a relaxing getaway to express gratitude if you're not the type to say it. The ideas are endless. Be as creative as you want or as simple as you can. Either way, know that your efforts will not go to waste.

I would also like to take this opportunity to publicly thank the core people in my life who have helped me become a better person every day and those who have never left my side since day one.

Dear God,

Hello, I'm back! It's me again. It has been a long time since I wrote you a letter. Don't worry, I will not rant or be angry at You this time. I have matured already, just so You know. Hehe. I want to thank You, dear God, for all the blessings that You have given me since the day I was born. I may not see you but I can always feel your presence. You allowed me to have a childhood so tough that I almost wanted to quit. Sure, there were a lot of challenges that I almost wanted to quit but You never fail to give me more reasons to have more faith in you during those times. One of which was knowing that You were training me to become a better person so I could be a better mom, wife, and daughter in the future. It was enough for me to persevere and hope my best despite the difficulties.

Thank You and I praise You endlessly for always providing for my needs; for ensuring my safety whenever I would cross the Olongapo highway; for giving me another opportunity to earn a living when being an actress didn't work for me; for sending Chito my way when I needed a best friend and a loving partner the most; and for trusting me with business ideas, partnerships, and opportunities so that people will have more jobs and they will have more chances to serve others as well.

Thank You for blessing me with a family that I never had. I promise to take care of them and raise them the best way Chito and I can. Thank you for Your shared wisdom. The Wais part in my being Wais Na Misis will always be credited to You, Lord.

Thank YOU.

Love,

Neri

———

Dear Mommy,

Don't worry, I am not writing to you to sneak out and join another school camping with my equally sneaky friends. But, I hope you have forgiven me for not only going against your will but also for taking two cans of Century Tuna from our cabinet to bring to camp without telling you. I promise to make up for it and take you out to dinner anywhere you like. But, may I suggest Amare, Jaytee's, Lime & Basil, or Jeju Samgyupsal? I heard they're the best. Hehehe.

I want to thank you for bringing me a whole grilled fish for me and my friends to share that night. I truly appreciate you for it because I was expecting a soap opera-worthy slap in my face but you gave me food instead.

Thank you, too, for not giving up on life even during the days when you desperately wanted to. We may not always see each other eye-to-eye and I may never understand your ways, but know that you are loved in spite of it all.

For your madiskarte *and Wais ways and for all the tough love you have given me—thank you. I will forever be grateful that you are my mommy.*

Love, Bunso

—

Dearest Chito,

No words can express how much I thank God for bringing you into my life. But, I will try to this time.

Thank you for all the days that you make me laugh. I swear I could get abs just by laughing with and at you every single day. You deliver the best punchlines, you let out the corniest dad jokes, and sometimes you just do nothing and it still makes me laugh.

Thank you for being there during my highs and most especially my lows. You never left my side and you continued to be there even when sometimes I didn't want you to. Thank you for endlessly pursuing me as if you are still courting me. I appreciate that, please don't ever change.

Let me also thank you for guiding me when I expressed interest in financial literacy and management. You have played a huge role in my being Wais Na Misis. Without you and your help, I wouldn't be as Wais as I am today.

I've said this before and I will never get tired of saying this again and again and again. You are the dream husband that every girl wants to have but I got to be the lucky one to have you all for myself.

Thank you for being the best father, the best husband, and most of all my best-est friend in the world.

I love you!

Love, Neri

—

To my forever babies Ate Pia, Kuya Miggy, and Baby Cash,

Mommy loves you THIIIIIIIIIIIIS MUCH! I keep telling God how thankful I am because He gave me you three. I cannot imagine my life without you guys in it. You make my world more colourful, more fun, and a bit more chaotic. But, that's okay. I love you three still.

Thank you Ate Pia for being a responsible big sister to your baby brothers. I appreciate the way you genuinely care for your brothers; how you patiently answer Miggy's uncountable questions; and the way you always try to be there when they need a playmate or a friend they can have fun with. I will always be proud of the person and amazing artist that you are and will become. Thank you for sharing your talents with us. I can't wait to see you soar!

Thank you Kuya Miggy for being you—the smart, witty, and talented little boy who brings so much happiness our way. Let me tell you how proud I am of the person you have become. You are such a sweet and artistic boy like your Ate Pia. I praise God for your life and your talents. Thank you for always wanting to join Mommy's early morning walks. I pray that you will still enjoy that, and we still get to do that even when you're older.

Thank you Cashypie for your overwhelming cuteness. Like your Kuya Miggy, you may not be able to understand what I'm telling you right now but know that I love you. I am excited to watch you grow and be with you and your siblings during the most important days of your lives. Well, I will also be there during the boring ones so you have no choice. You're still a baby as of this writing so I can't say much but I love you and thank you for coming into our lives. You can eat all the pancit (noodles) *that you want in this lifetime. I promise you that.*

Love, Mommy

—

My Dear Ninang Mace,

Thank you for taking care of me when I was starting out as an actress. I remember the days when I was still trying to make it in the industry, you were there with me every step of the way. You laughed, cried, got hungry, and fought bullies with me.

Now, you are helping me raise my kids and loving them like they're your own. Thank you for being you, my best friend, and my number one kakampi (ally).

A thank you letter may not be enough for all the years that you have been with me and for the support that you have extended to my family. But, this will do for now. I feel so blessed to have you in our lives. I pray that God will bless you more because you have the biggest heart, the gentlest hands, and the kindest soul.

Thank you for everything that you do. We promise to take care of you as well as you are taking care of us. We are your family.

Love, Neri

—

Hi, Dad!

There's so much I want to tell you but let me simply thank you for everything that you have done for me and my siblings. We may not have the best father-and-daughter relationship but I will always be grateful for the happy memories with you. The kinds of stories that I will always share with my children when they're older.

I never got to see you before you passed but I hope you know that I have forgiven you a long long time ago. With that, I pray that wherever you are, may you be at peace.

Thank you for the wonderful memories, Dad. 'Til I see you again!

Love,

Bunso

—

Dear Wais Na Misis,

Thank you for picking up this book and for trusting me to help you at this moment in your life. You don't know how much I am grateful for your never-ending support and love not just for me but for my whole family as well. Because of your unending trust, I have learned how to trust in myself more, too.

I know I still have a lot to learn, but thank you for being with me on this journey.

I am grateful for your patience and understanding, most especially on days when life becomes a bit more challenging for me and my family.

I thank God for your life and I pray that you be blessed with even more wisdom than I have so you can also help make this world an even better place for our children and the future generations to live in.

Love, Neri

—

Dear Neri,

Hello, self. What's up? I just want to acknowledge and thank you for making it this far. You still have a long way to go but with God and your determination, I know you will make it. Know that I am proud of you. You are doing great. Heartaches and challenges will always be a part of life so don't worry about them too much.

I am grateful that you are doing your best even on the days when you think you are not.

Thank you, ten-year-old Neri, for not giving up. I know you didn't exactly have an awesome childhood but now that you're older, I hope you see why you were given those hardships. God has been with you all these years, you see. He hasn't left your side. So, I thank and praise Him, too!

Big big thanks to you, Neri, for keeping a calm and contented heart when the world tried to tear you down. I appreciate you for always trying to see the good in every situation (of course with boundaries!)—even the ones that are ugly and painful.

You are going great. Keep on doing it because that's what God wants you to do in your life. I've said this once, I'll say it again: Thank you, Neri, for not giving up.

Until the next business venture!

Love,

Neri

PART 3: With My Family, It's Always tWAIS the Fun!

Chapter 11

My Childhood Dream

You would have easily believed me if I told you that my childhood dream was to become a doctor, a lawyer, a scientist, an astronaut, or a Hollywood celebrity. These are all great dreams to have, don't get me wrong. They might even be among the top answers to a Family Feud question. But, for some unexplainable reason, not one of them popped in my head when I had my Dear God moment at around seven years old (I was in the first grade, to be precise).

My childhood dream was to become a mom and a housewife. This I am sure of because I remember writing it in my diary.

I've always known and felt that my seven-year-old self loved loving people. And I must've felt., that becoming a mother was the most legitimate and convincing way to achieve this God-given desire without anyone questioning my intentions. After all, though differently, I grew up seeing how my mother operated with the idea of love. Hers was just the kind of motherhood that wasn't ideal but I've seen her embody her role in the best way she knew.

I also used to think that mothers were like MacGyvers (say hello to another 90s pop culture icon reference. I'll save you the time, kids. *MacGyver* is a popular television show that aired in 1985 and continued until around the early 2000s. He's an all-around guy who can practically solve all problems and wiggle his way out of any obstacle with whatever available item he had at hand. Think of him as the Swiss Army knife personified.), because that was how my mom was. What she lacked in the emotional department, she definitely made up for it with her street smart and survival skills. Hand her anything and she could sell it like a pro. Whenever things would conk out at home and we had no money to pay for a handyman, she would do her best to try to fix it herself. I have seen her reassemble a broken faucet; mend our torn shirts; attach a doorknob; and stabilize an old wobbly table.

That was what I knew of the role, thus the childhood dream. Then I grew up ... and eventually became a mom. Do I still see it the same way? You may ask.

Truth be told, the 'loving people' aspect of being one, still holds true. But I have realized that being a mother takes more than just loving people. Like any other dream job, it is a good mix of God's grace, coupled with hard work and a lot of trial and error to become even close to better at what we do.

The point here is: now that I have become one, I found out that there is another side to motherhood than just building a home and raising a family. It isn't purely rainbows and daisies, and it isn't a walk in the park either.

So before I dive into the chapters discussing family life, I have decided to dedicate one, solely to understanding the challenging yet wonderful world of motherhood. I want to share my learnings and realizations with you so we can all be better teammates and allies to our mothers no matter how good or bad they may have treated us in the past.

Because for me, being a Wais Na Misis doesn't just mean being a master of a lot of skills. It also means having the awareness and understanding that we need to be looking beyond what people usually choose to show us so we can extend empathy and compassion. This will also help others to make sense of the things . . . that they are going through, something more often than not, they choose not to express.

This chapter is for all the mommas in the world. This is also for the husbands, the children, the best friends, and the rest of her tribe around her.

WAIS TIP #32: REMEMBER THAT MOMS ARE HUMANS, TOO

We often look like we are always on top of things—not missing a schedule, and not a hair out of place. I guess that comes with the territory. After all, culture has always portrayed moms as a kind who should be almost close to perfection—one of the two main people in the family who must always stay strong.

But we are not. WE CANNOT BE STRONG ALL THE TIME and the world must understand that. As much as you see us smiling and having fun with our kids or while shopping for tonight's dinner, we sometimes feel the opposite when unfavourable circumstances overshadow because we are humans like the rest of you. We get hungry, we feel tired, and we become grumpy, too. Yes, I know some moms can express their emotions and needs well. But, there are those too who, like my mom, cannot articulate what is inside their hearts and so they resort to silence or, sadly, violence. Now, please know that I do not tolerate and support the latter. I am just sharing my personal experiences of how I was made to understand that there really are people like my mom who were victims of circumstances that are out of their control. Because she didn't know how to process her emotions, she unknowingly passed on her hurt to her children. Specifically me.

I remember vividly the time when my mom would patiently finish cross-stitch projects featuring my face and call her masterpiece 'Princess Neri'. She must have secretly adored me for her to constantly have my face recreated using threads, not once but thrice or more. She also had big dreams for us which showed in her choices as we were growing up. She took us to Baguio to settle there so we could get the chance to study in a better school. She did everything she could to make ends meet while my dad was abroad. She was a huge supporter of my career and businesses, too.

And then there were days, most especially when I was younger, when she would become violent towards me. There were times when would slap me so hard that I thought my eyeballs had popped out of their sockets. She often did this when she wasn't in the mood to answer my questions about some things that were happening within our family. She used to curse me, too. She'd push me away when I'd sit beside her during one of her *mahjong* games because she believed I was the reason why she would always lose.

I won't deny that the things she did hurt me. They were all traumatizing. But, eventually, I found out that during the times when she would sometimes unknowingly inflict pain on me, she had been silently suffering too. At that time, she shared that she had been carrying the burden of knowing that my dad had been getting more and more addicted to drugs until it consumed him. All his earnings and savings were carelessly spent on his friends who also took illegal substances with him.

My mom tried to act as if nothing frustrating was happening because she said she didn't want us to worry. She also decided to keep the issue to herself so we don't hold any grudge against our dad. Until the very end, she wanted to protect him for reasons unknown to us.

My point here is that at times our moms are suffering or carrying a burden that's beyond their capacity, no matter how frustrating or annoying they get at some point. So, as a Wais person, instead of the natural response to retaliate and hurt back what they've inflicted on us, let's try to extend a little more kindness and patience toward moms and other people in general when they start to become less than their usual bubbly selves. Don't take it against them if they express exhaustion or anger. Instead, try to look beyond it and simply understand. Because like babies, moms cry, grieve, and feel all sorts of unhappy emotions, too, and that's perfectly okay. However, if things get out of hand, it is not wrong, to set boundaries too, and slowly distance yourself so as not to create more conflict.

WAIS TIP #33: THEY WERE SOMEONE BEFORE THEY WERE 'MOM'

'To you, Mom was always Mom. It never occurred to you that she had once taken her first step, or had once been three or twelve or twenty years old. Mom was Mom. She was born as Mom. Until you saw her running to your uncle like that, it hadn't dawned on you that she was a human being who harboured the exact same feeling you had for your own brothers, and this realization led to the awareness that she, too, had had a childhood. From then on, you sometimes thought of Mom as a child, as a girl, as a young woman, as a newlywed, as a mother who had just given birth to you.'

This line from Kyung Sook-Shin's book titled *Please Look After Mother* greatly inspired this Wais Tip. After reading the book, I remembered being affected by it for days. It stirred something in me that made me think of my mom and what her life was like before she had us. I didn't know who my mom really was before I called her Mommy. I had little to no idea about her childhood or the kind of environment she grew up in. All I know is that she is a woman of few words. She also wasn't able to finish grade school but she knows how to read and write. When she was still single, she lived with some of her siblings and helped their families. Those were the only pre-mommy stories I know of.

Sometimes I couldn't help but imagine what she was as a teenager. Did she experience having crushes, too? I wondered who were the celebrities she liked during her time and what kinds of mischief she did when she was younger.

My mom's seventy-three now and her anger towards me has mellowed down. She's a lot calmer and more open to trying out new things with us. Her new disposition came with the consideration that if there will be days when my mom will prefer to be on her own or to do the things that interest her but without us, I would just let her be. After all, being a mother is a non-stop job and a lifetime commitment. In fact, it can help us become better partners and mothers when we are given a chance to breathe and pursue our personal interests, too.

WAIS TIP #34: MOMS LOVE IT WHEN SOMEONE LOOKS AFTER THEM, TOO

If you now have the chance to spend a little extra time on or money for your mom, have you treated her to dinner lately? Have you given into their cute floral bouquet or out-of-town trip requests? Were you able to visit her when she asked you to? Whatever your mom's preferred love language may be, if it is in your power to spoil her, do it. Life is short.

As much as the abovementioned gestures are nice to do and experience, I completely understand that some of you may not have a good relationship with your moms, so please feel free to skip this part of the book. You have your reasons and I respect that.

My mom may have given me a slightly traumatic childhood but it doesn't erase the fact that her entire body and spirit have been altered forever just by simply pushing us four (of course not simultaneously!) out into the world from inside her body. Knowing the irreversible change that my siblings and I have caused her was more than enough for me to strive to repay her sacrifices and spoil her whenever I can. And the fact that I will not have her forever drives me to make the remaining days of her life extra special.

So whenever I get a chance, I take her to our farm or to the beach so she could breathe in the fresh air. Since she only lives a few minutes away from me, I sometimes also ask Chito to drop by the house we bought for her to bring her food whenever he's on his way home from work. I would also bring her to our home on special days so she could play and spend time with her grandchildren. These little gestures may never be enough to repay all the sacrifices, tough love, and hard work she has done for us but I make sure to make the most of our time together whenever possible.

WAIS TIP #35: KNOW THAT NO MOTHER IS THE SAME. NEVER COMPARE

I have something to confess. There were days when I wished I had a different mother. I was young and probably didn't know any better so I assumed that all moms should be gentle and dedicated to their children all the time.

But, as with all the other realizations I've had growing up, this too, has opened my eyes to the fact that no two moms are the same. Each has her own unique set of experiences that they bring with them into the relationship with their partners and the children. This uniqueness in perspective and personality helps shaping the way she interacts with and raises her family. Motherhood is a deeply emotional and personal experience that involves a huge part, if not the whole, of a woman's being.

My mom was a believer of tough love while I am a 'touch-love' kind of mom. Because I grew up in a non-affectionate home, one that could rival the military, I ensure that I balance everything out with my family. I hug my kids and tell them how much I love them whenever I can. But, I also don't hold back on a stern reprimand (with explanation) when needed.

Let me end this chapter with a reminder that being a mother is not a competition but a journey. Every mother deserves respect, love, and understanding for whoever we may be before becoming a mom; whatever backgrounds we may have come from; and whatever set of beliefs we may have grown up with. I didn't exactly have a healthy relationship with my mom when I was growing up but I still chose to give her the same respect. I believe there should be boundaries set for mothers who may not be 'decent and honourable', and who may be 'toxic' for the family, but respect should always be given to everyone.

Chapter 12

Partnering with God's Best

In this chapter, I will be sharing some personal anecdotes from me and my husband, Chito, as we do our best to raise a healthy family together. I am used to conquering life alone. Now that I have him, I am so happy to have discovered more of married-life learnings and I am excited to share the best ones with you. I know that there will definitely be some tips and tricks that you may already be aware of. Just skip those and leave it to the ones who are still trying to learn it. Maybe use it as a reminder in case you have forgotten it, or if it got buried in your grocery lists … or your children's mountain of toys!

WAIS TIP #36: YOUR SPOUSE IS YOUR BEST TEAMMATE

I consider Chito and my marriage a lot like committing to a team sport. We won't win, and we won't reach our goals unless we choose to work together. When it comes to raising a family, Chito is still the head of the pack. But, in running a household and making sure that the family is well-fed and everything at home is spick and span, it is me who takes the lead. It's basically a give-and-take relationship. We respect each other's roles by giving each other space to effectively fulfil the tasks but, we also don't hesitate to holler for one another whenever we encounter roadblocks or whenever one of us gets tied up with work.

As with any other team sport, you and your partner should have clear roles and positions at home so your household runs smoothly.

In one of our interviews for *Metro.Style*, a Philippine-based online lifestyle magazine, Chito had this to say about our dynamics: *Lahat kami team players dito. Okay 'yung mga staff namin dito. Pero si Neri talaga siya*

talaga ang—homemaker ba tawag doon? So, she handles everything! She makes
sure na everything is maayos. Pareho kaming OC-OC sa ganyan. So, si Neri is
always on her toes kasi ayoko ng makalat. So, she tries her best na ganu'n din. Siya
talaga, siya talaga. Ang division, ako, support lang ako whenever she has work I
try my best to take care of Miggy para hindi siya kulitin and makapag-focus siya
sa work. Or, 'pag pagod siya, lalaruin ko si Miggy para makapagpahinga siya.
Kasi aside from that, siya talaga nakatutok for that. So ako, ang role ko talaga
dito is Miggy's playmate! So, I try to make sure nakakapag-rest siya, I always ask
her if she wants coffee, or tea or basta kung gusto niyang magpahinga. I try my best
to take care of her. (We are all team players here. Our staff is okay, too.
But, Neri is really the—homemaker, is this what it's called? She handles
everything! She makes sure that everything's in its proper place. We are
both OC-OC when it comes to that. Neri is always on her toes because
I do not like it when the house is messy.

She tries her best to keep it clean. It's her, all because of her. Our
division of labour at home is that I take the supporting role whenever
she has work. I try my best to take care of Miggy and make sure he
doesn't bother her so she can focus on her work. Or, when she's
exhausted I play with Miggy so she can fully rest. Because aside from
her work, she is really the one on top of things at home. My real role
here is Miggy's playmate! So, I try to make sure that she is able to rest.
I always ask her if she wants coffee, or tea, or if she just wants to take
a rest. I try my best to take care of her.)

Apart from helping each other succeed and performing our tasks
well, as teammates, we are also each other's first line of defense. We
protect each other as much as we protect the rest of our family. Our
problems are ours to experience and solve and our shortcomings are
never given the space on our social media pages.

I have learned from my mom that refraining from exposing your
spouse's flaws, the things he did wrong, and the many things that
annoy you about him, isn't an act of martyrdom. Rather, it's a show
of commitment to the person you chose to spend the rest of your life
with. Keeping your business to yourselves also allows you two to . . .

Build trust. Dealing with your issues privately creates a special
bond between you two so do your best to cooperate with each other
despite the differences. When you do the opposite, your partner may

feel betrayed or dehumanized. If he finds out that you have shared your problems in public, this might become a reason why he will start to keep secrets from you, instead of opening up, for fear of being judged. If you are caught up in a heated argument, give yourselves some time to cool down first before trying to discuss the problem.

Maintain respect. I truly believe that there's no relationship if respect doesn't exist within it. I'd rather not be in a relationship than be in one without respect for each other. You are teammates, for better or for worse, so posting about your husband's flaws or ranting about him on social media out of frustration and anger can be humiliating for him no matter how horrible his sins were. If it's that grave of an offence, take it to court or the police, or to anyone who can do something about it. Not in a place where your relationship with him can be the subject of more judgment and gossip.

Make room for improvement. Because only the two of you know each other's flaws, you both have more headspace and freedom to make things right. There are no unnecessary opinions or unsolicited comments that might potentially cloud your judgment and make everything worse.

Honour your commitment. When you are faced with a tough situation, the part where you promised to be with your spouse for better or for worse, in front of God, comes into play. It's our problem, we are given that challenge, so it's up to us to solve it. When we know we can't handle it, we leave it to God because He is more powerful and capable to solve it than any of the people on social media. I believe this is also a wise move than letting relatives or friends influence us into a decision that we might regret later. We are all flawed humans after all.

Bottomline is, try to focus on the good that might come out of the situation. I'm not in any way promoting toxic positivity, don't get me wrong. All I'm saying is that there will always be hope. Offer your situation to God and shift your energy into improving your relationship by using the ugly experiences as stepping stones and not as blocks to throw at your husband's face out of annoyance.

WAIS TIP #37: BALANCE EACH OTHER OUT

Chito is an artist: a musician, skillful at drawing, and an overall creative person. Because of this, his personality tends to be more on the emotional side. Since artists are often deeply in touch with their feelings, it comes as no surprise that Chito is a lot like this, too; making him confrontational and intensely vocal about his thoughts and feelings. He's the type to voice out and express whatever he is strongly feeling right then and there.

Chito is also the type to share his innermost thoughts, even explaining in detail why he is feeling what he is feeling. While I am the total opposite. I am the quiet type of person who would just choose to deal with her emotions on her own. I grew up with the strong conviction that no one can solve any of my problems except for God and myself. I see no reason why I need to broadcast every difficult thing that I go through when the solution can be found someplace else or even within me. Though sometimes, I recognize too that people share their problems because they simply want someone to listen.

Still, I was and still am the type to try to keep things and deal with them myself.

Chito and I never clashed during the early days of our relationship. In fact, it was only when I became busy with being a hands-on mother and entrepreneur that we started to. Blame exhaustion paired with hormonal imbalance.

So, whenever Chito and I would argue, he would pour his heart out and I would remain silent until the end. Once the argument's over, that would be the only time I would calmly share a few of my thoughts and proceed to resolve the problem at hand. For me, this was and still is the best way. But I was surprised when one day my best friend and Chito told me, on different occasions, to let out my anger even just once because I rarely do.

So when I had the chance, I told Chito this: *'Kung galit ka at galit din ako, mag-aaway lang tayo. Makakapagsalita tayo ng mga words that we don't mean at baka may magawa pa tayong ikaka-regret natin.'* (When we are both angry, we are just going to fight. We are going to say words that we don't mean and we may even do things that we both might regret.)

Because of this, we have resolved to help each other out by being each other's check and balance. I keep this in mind, too, whenever I would face a problem of my own. I still don't like showing extremely negative emotions but now that I have finally understood that it's okay to feel and express it sometimes, I now would consult with Chito first. I'd share with him the situation and ask him what should be my best response to it.

It's the same way for him. He must have taken notes about the way I handle my problems and emotions because he would also now try to calm himself first before he deals with whatever challenge is facing him.

The check and balance dynamics also applies when we are making business decisions. He is a conservative businessman while I am the risk taker. We compare notes and analyse the pros and cons first before finalizing a decision. Chito would also be the first person I'd turn to, for example, if there's something I need to buy for our businesses or if there's a business that I want to pursue. I would lay out all the details for him and he would help me analyse everything. He would ask me questions as if I were doing my thesis defense to help me narrow down all my options and make sure that all bases are covered. When everything's clear, only then would he allow me to make the final decision based on what we have discussed through his guidance.

To further illustrate how we check and balance each other, Chito would often share in his interviews that we have different ways of raising our kids, too. For him, I am the stricter parent. I am aware of it because he would sometimes tell me '*Wag ganyan ka strict. Dapat relax lang.*' (Don't be too strict. You should just be relaxed). Sometimes, too, he would make fun of my being a disciplinarian whenever he'd use me to scare Miggy when he becomes a little too naughty. He'd tell him jokingly, 'Oh, you want me to call mommy? Behave or I'll call mommy.' And surprisingly, Miggy would stop whatever mischief he was doing and sit still.

However, jokes aside, I also made sure that Chito understands that being a strict mom isn't something to be used as a scare tactic because being strict for logical reasons brings peace and order to a home.

WAIS TIP #38: LAUGHTER IS STILL THE BEST MEDICINE!

This part I have proven true so many times in our relationship. It sounds cliché but believe me, there is nothing that a round of laughter cannot fix. I thank God for making my husband witty, funny, and crazy. I laugh even when he isn't doing anything.

While it can't obviously fix your broken faucet or sew back your torn carpet, laughter can help lighten the mood and cushion the blow for when things get a little heated.

Sometimes, too, even if there's nothing to mend, simply laughing with your partner can make the entire feel of your home lighter and brighter. This can result in better dynamics and stronger connections.

I thank God, again, that one of my husband's superpowers is his unbelievable sense of humour. When we started dating, his humour and his impressive punchline deliveries were among the things that he did that made me feel comfortable around him. He is seven years older than me and his family background is the total opposite of mine, but we instantly clicked because I was just soooo happy and I was always laughing that I didn't mind our differences any more.

He's also a lot like Mr Bean, another 90s icon known for his funny antics and childish comedic acts. Without speaking a word, Mr Bean made his audience laugh through his facial expressions or the way he would interact with random people in the show.

That's what Chito is like, for me. Sometimes he would do nothing. He would be just standing or sitting at a spot and I would immediately find him funny, and laugh.

Other days, he would simply blurt out a statement or he'd just randomly say something and it would leave me laughing like crazy.

I remember there was one time we went out on a date at a fine-dining restaurant in Tagaytay. I wore a comfy dress and Chito, who had probably forgotten about the dress code, wore a casual polo shirt and a pair of shorts. It was only after we left our house that we realized we might not be able to enter the restaurant because of his shorts. We could've easily argued about it or the inconvenience might have ruined our night but Chito's humour swooped in at the right time. He said, *'PhP5,000 ang bili ko sa shorts, baka pasado na 'yun!'* (I bought the shorts for PhP5,000. Maybe they'll allow it!"). With this, we ended up laughing as we went back home so he could change.

We got to the restaurant in time for our reservation, thank goodness! While we were seated and waiting for our food, we were served small pieces of bread, two half pieces to be exact. This made Chito jokingly ask *'Bakit hati tayo sa bread? Eh ang mahal mahal dito, bakit nagtitipid sila sa tinapay?'* (Why are we sharing the bread? The restaurant's pretty expensive, why are they so stingy with the bread?) Instead of being *HANGRY,* we ended up laughing 'til our bellies ached. In hindsight, it was good enough that our bellies ached because of laughter and not because of hunger. The latter would've been a disaster.

Our date went well and we ate to our heart's content. We also had a good conversation in between. When it was time to pay for our meal, Chito saw another opening to let out a punchline that I was pretty sure had been brewing in his head the entire time. He might be just waiting for the right timing.

When the bill was handed to him, I saw him ask the staff in a poker-faced, humorous manner if he could pay in installments but for six months. Now, if you know my husband, you are probably aware of how he lets out a joke or two with a straight face even when the people around him are starting to break into laughter. I could've been easily embarrassed by what he had done because we had money to pay for what we ate, to begin with. Other guests may have judged us for this, too. But he delivered the punchline so well that I, and the rest of the guests at the nearby table, couldn't help but laugh as well.

I also remember that one time Chito asked me to accompany him to go buy something. Since I had just finished my first work for the day and I had a two-hour free time until my next one, I quickly agreed. He went downstairs while I remained in our room to prepare. When I got down, there was no car or a husband in sight. I instinctively tried to reach him via his mobile phone but he forgot to bring it with him.

Well, he must've realized he'd forgotten his wife so he came back for me. He was apologetic. I just couldn't help but laugh because Chito has a way of injecting humour in everything that he does, so much so that it helps improve whatever kind of situation we are in. I mean I could've been annoyed that he had wasted my time because I could've done something worthwhile than to prepare for the trip he wanted to bring me on. But, again, his sense of humour and his quick wit to turn things around for the better have made all the difference.

While humour may not be considered as one of the most important reasons why a marriage or a relationship becomes successful, I can confidently say that it plays a huge role in creating a happy, comfortable, and trusting environment for the couple.

When you pray and ask God for the best partner for you, don't forget to ask for one who, not only has a great personality but a great sense of humour, too. Trust me, you won't regret it.

WAIS TIP #39: NEVER STOP PURSUING YOUR SPOUSE

If you follow us on our social media pages, I'm pretty sure you have seen some of our posts about each other. And I know, for those looking from the outside in, our posts may sometimes make you cringe. We understand that.

But, from our perspective, our posts dedicated to each other aren't exactly done just to show off or to make up for something wrong we had done. We post about each other occasionally because that's one of the ways we keep the fire of our relationship burning. I shouldn't be explaining myself here, but I just want to share that in this era of social media, that is one surefire way of making your significant other feel special. It's one of the languages of this generation, don't be afraid to speak it.

Having said that, it's okay, too, if that isn't your thing. My point here is that if you have been blessed with a partner, do your best to keep your love alive. Your courtship shouldn't end on the day you said yes to being his girlfriend or his wife. It should continue even after the lovey-dovey stage gets over because that's where the real adventure begins and where your love and affection will greatly be needed. For the men who are reading this, know that making your wife feel special and loved in every little way that you can think of makes a huge difference. She may be feeling sad or suffering from things that she won't outrightly tell you about. So, your act of pursuing her and continuously trying to win her heart will definitely heal her in more ways than you can imagine.

May I share with you something? As cheesy and cringey as it may sound to some of you but Chito loves giving me letters and filling my inbox with sweet nothings.

Sometimes he does this too when we have just come out of a fight. Words are his love language and he makes sure he is able to make me feel loved through them.

No matter what your love language is for your spouse, keep on using it and use it well.

Chapter 13

Raising Ate Pia, Kuya Miggy, Cash, and . . . Chito

I have been asked one too many times what is my mom-life like, now that I have three kids plus my honourary eldest, Chito, to raise. I can honestly say, it is nothing like my childhood daydreams, as those were easy and it was a fun world to live in. At times, my reality now is tiring and challenging. But, I can confidently say that what I have now is even better than the kind of life I had dreamt of.

Having the privilege of building a family and raising kids who are mini-versions of Chito and me, are among the top things that I will forever be thanking God for. I could've just grown as a single woman, travelling the world, or working my way up the corporate ladder but I guess God had a different plan for me. Not only did He give me the grace to live a life, long enough to experience my dream of becoming a mom but He also entrusted me with a lovely family to serve and care for.

Sure, there are inevitable hard times. But the good always outweighs the bad, at least that's how I'd like to always see life. And just like what Chito would always proclaim in his vlogs and interviews, having a family brings us so much joy. It's like we have this permanent and constant set of friends who we are destined to make sure are happy, safe, and healthy. The kind that makes everything in life so simple. The choice is easy because they will always be the answers.

WAIS TIP #40: TREAT YOUR CHILDREN AS YOUR FRIENDS

I know that this WAIS TIP is something that may or may not work for some families so proceed with caution. But because I grew up with parents who created a huge gap and drew rather obvious boundaries between us, I knew what kind of an environment it would create if I replicate the same strategy and apply it on my own family. So instead of going through the traditional 'I'm the parent and you're just my child' route, I took a different path to try and become their friend.

At first, I was hesitant because I worried about having difficulty setting boundaries and keeping our authority as parents if we enjoy being their friends a little too much. But, I thank God that Chito and I were able to strike a balance that worked for our family and my children's specific needs. Building a friendship with our children is a rewarding experience but our role as parents always comes first. We discipline them as much as we enjoy their company.

It's still too early to tell but with the brief trial and error we've had, we have learned that ...

1. **Listening is as valuable as talking.** When Pia and Miggy share their innermost thoughts and feelings with me, I pause whatever it is that I am doing and take the time to listen actively and make them feel that I value whatever it is that they have to say. If there is an emergency, I will drop everything to be with them immediately. Because when I was young I wasn't exactly heard or attended to by my parents, and that made me feel helpless and alone. I do not want my children to ever feel the same way. So, as much as possible I make active listening a vital part of our communication process.

2. **Sharing our experiences as a child helps them comprehend the lessons we are trying to teach them.** There was one time I was making Miggy understand why he has to appreciate everything that he has right now. Of course, he is just a little boy with limited knowledge about the world so I had to patiently illustrate, through my childhood stories, why he has to think that way. Instead of telling him as it is, I painted a picture in his mind by sharing with him that when I was younger, we didn't have enough money to even buy a burger from a fast-food restaurant. And it was only

during high school that I got to savour my first taste of a famous fast-food meal. He must've finally understood the idea because he felt so sorry for me after hearing the story.

3. **Finding common interests build a friendship.** Because I wanted to spend more time with them and get to know them deeper, I made sure to look for and do something that would also spark their interest. Miggy and I enjoy gardening, baking, and cooking together and similarly, I have so much fun cooking and baking with Ate Pia. Now, we are trying to learn pottery and other activities that the kids would want to try; set up a bonfire and camp around it while eating our homemade smores and grilled meats; rediscover our neighbouring cities while indulging in nature sightseeing; and taking road trips within our area as a family without gadgets. We also make sure that whatever the kids want, Chito and I are always with them exploring and experiencing life together. It sounds challenging but we are having so much fun!

4. **Respecting boundaries is not only for adults.** Children are smarter than we give them credit for. I grew up in an era when children were sometimes regarded as little humans who had no control over their minds and bodies; and who had no say in their lives just because they were mere children. When I was younger and my mom would ask me to do something, my answer was always a trembling YES or a hesitant YES because a sharp slap in the face awaited me each time I would say NO. She never explained to me why I was supposed to do something, so I simply blindly obeyed. Looking back, my boundaries were crossed one too many times which eventually made me function out of fear and despise from where I was at. I didn't want that to happen to my own family, so even if they are still young, Chito and I talk to them and give them the same respect as we would give any adult that we would encounter. Because of these, I saw how my kids have developed this certain confidence and trust in us, and it made our home an even better and safer place to live in.

WAIS TIP #41: JUST BECAUSE WE ARE ADULTS DOESN'T MEAN WE ARE ALWAYS RIGHT

Chito and I aren't parenting experts but we have been parents long enough for us to realize that just because we are THE parents doesn't automatically give us the green light to be right all the time. I had that kind of experience with my own parents. Since mine weren't progessive, I made sure to reverse the traditional idea and turn it into a progressive one, at least for our family.

When we run into a misunderstanding, we make sure that we validate their emotions. We don't shrug off what they are feeling just because we assume that things could've been worse. It is our responsibility as parents to listen to what they have to say and patiently sit with them as they process their thoughts and emotions.

As I help them navigate their complex feelings, we both learn from the experience. There are times when I'd find myself in the wrong so I would sincerely apologize to my child and let them know how sorry I am. This, in turn, makes them see that I am their ally and that apologizing does not make anyone any less of a person.

Doing this encourages them to do the same.

This also applies to the kinds of dreams we might have for our children. I grew up with my mom creating my dreams for me. For the longest time, it was she who had wanted me to try out and audition to become an actress because it was her dream for me to become a celebrity. As I have mentioned before, maybe this was also the reason why she'd always push me to join beauty contests so that at least I could get a shot at stardom. Having this experience, I vowed not to do the same to my kids as it can backfire. Instead of encouraging my kids to pursue their own dreams they might be discouraged or confused, and that might make them stop pursuing anything in the long run.

Go easy on your kids. Allow them to discover whatever it is that they are good at and simply guide them once they do. God has a blueprint for every human being He has created. Trust Him and your child to discover it together. You'll be surprised!

WAIS TIP #42: SHOW YOUR CHILDREN THE WORLD AND TRAIN THEM FOR LIFE

One of these days, my children will leave us to build their own families. That's a fact. So as early as now, we make sure that everything is in order—from their savings to their investments and overall well-being. It's not that I am spoiling them or spoon-feeding them so much that I leave no room for them to decide on their own. I simply want to give them a good start so that by the time comes when they won't be needing us any more, they can make it through life with ease.

We make sure that our kids are equipped to deal with almost anything that life may throw at them. We usually start with the simplest ones like being with them outdoors and letting them explore the world to their heart's content. In line with this, we also limit their gadget and screen exposure to as little time as possible. It's too early for them to become too dependent on technology.

We try and encourage them to try as many activities as they would want and support them in every possible way. Just like when my eldest, Ate Pia, showed interest in the arts and music. I tried to enroll her in voice lessons and bought her an iPad where she can continue to create her impressive digital art (you should check it out on my Instagram and Facebook accounts, as well as her own Instagram page sometime!). When I saw Miggy had a talent for the arts, too, I immediately bought him large sheets of paper, blank canvasses, and tons of paints that he can experiment with. I don't mind the mess that he makes each time he feels inspired to paint. As long as he can express what's inside that creative brain of his, I fully support him.

Chito loves introducing new types of food that aren't usually fed to kids their age like *taho* and *balut*. He said he didn't want them to become picky eaters like he was when he was their age as it gave him a hard time when he grew older. It was only then that he was able to fully appreciate eating vegetables and other types of food that he once found unsavoury.

And I love showing them the beauty of the outdoors and sharing with them my love for gardening. I allow them to get their hands dirty and be really exposed to it. I make them till the soil, scoop out fertilizers, plant and bury the seeds, and harvest the crops using their own hands.

Chito and I do everything with our kids with full confidence in what the Bible says about training up a child in the way he should go, so when he is old he will not depart from it. We train them as early as now with the hope that our children will become better people, even better than we are in the future.

WAIS TIP #43: HEAL, SO YOU DON'T RAISE BROKEN CHILDREN

We all have issues. We are mere humans with many uncontrollable events happening with us which is why awareness of the fact that we need healing is of great importance. I understand that not everyone's given the chance to heal just in time to raise a family. But when you get one, don't think twice and grab it!

Healing, be it physical, spiritual, mental, or emotional, can help us process and overcome past traumas and unresolved emotions. And as parents, when we don't heal from our emotional wounds, we can unintentionally pass on the pain and trauma to our children through our parenting styles and how we interact with them on a day-to-day basis. This, in turn, can create a cycle of dysfunction that can possibly harm future generations if not attended to properly.

I thank God for His grace because if not for it, I might not have the awareness, strength, and wisdom to start a new story for my family. There are many ways to heal and it will vary from one situation to another so I cannot suggest an exact set of steps that you can follow. However, I can always share what has greatly helped and contributed to my healing. Know that healing isn't a one-time thing. It is a continuous process in which I am still involved, bit by bit. Here are some of the things I have been consciously doing for faster and better healing:

1. **I pray a lot.** I am fully aware that this battle against trauma isn't just mine to fight but God's as well. And because I know that He is powerful and more capable to bring changes and help in healing than I do, I surrender everything to Him through my constant

prayers. I also ask God to show me the next steps that I should take so I can heal faster and better.

2. **I surround myself with people who are good for my overall health.** And as much as possible, I stay away from people who love to gossip or tear other people down. We don't need that kind of energy.

3. **I keep myself healthy** by regularly brisk walking in the morning and eating nutritious foods, which are mostly from my backyard garden.

4. **I practice self-care** by resting when my body feels tired and attending to its needs whenever I feel like it's about to give up. I don't deprive myself of self-care activities like going to ExtraordiNERI salon for haircuts and hair colour. I also treat myself to sumptuous food by eating at one of my restaurants or cooking at home. Lastly, I go easy on myself and others as well.

5. **I forgive.** As much as my natural tendencies prevent me from doing so, I try my best to still do it. It's hard, I know because we are just humans. So again, I seek God's help so I can forgive even the hardest and most painful of offences. I have also realized that I will gain nothing if I hold grudges against the people who have wronged me. In fact, it will make me their prisoner and that will prevent me from living a positive and stress-free life. Why would I want that, right? Forgiving releases me from the unnecessary burden which makes it easier for me to receive help and jumpstart my healing. However, I also do not disregard the fact that as much as I want to forgive and move on, I also need to protect myself and my family by setting boundaries. If the person I have forgiven has been proven to be toxic and unhealthy to be around us, I do not hesitate to set boundaries. If the person becomes too much, I do not think twice about cutting it off if needed.

Chapter 14

Homemaking Hacks

We have now arrived at one of the most fun parts of being a wife and a mom (at least for me!). It's quite obvious by now that I love taking care of my family. Everything about it excites me and makes me feel most alive. But if you ask me which one takes the cake, I'd say it's homemaking. Some people would consider it a luxury, a privilege even, that not a lot can afford. Because in this fast-paced world, creating a warm, inviting, and functional home is something that's not really a priority since it will take so much of our time, money, and effort.

I have also looked at it that way at one point. Coming from an underprivileged background, I literally had nothing in mind but to work work and then work some more. I didn't care if the kind of place I'd go to is welcoming or if it would just look like any other four-walled space with a bed to sleep on. However, when I started to have my own condo I realized that hey, having a nice place that's livable, systematic, and cozy has a significant effect on my overall well-being. I seldom woke up grumpy; I looked forward to the days when I'd shop for bargain items to decorate my place; and cleaning and maintaining my space surprisingly gave me a certain kind of peace and calm within me that I didn't find it tiring when I had to do it all over again.

Now that I have a family and a bigger home to take care of, my homemaking skills have evolved, too. What used to work for me when I was living on my own had to be tweaked to accommodate my growing family.

Anyway, let me stop right here. I don't want to make you wait any longer. May I present to you some of my homemaking hacks that I hope you get to learn from. Have fun!!!

WAIS TIP #44: START A 'HOME MANAGEMENT' PLANNER

I have notebooks for anything and everything so I don't forget. I also keep one when it comes to managing my household because I like to be on top of things and I don't like missing out on a single detail. That's how much I value and love my family.

In my 'Home Management Plan' notebook, I have my family's daily and weekly schedule that I use as a guide for the day. But because I am aware that even the strictest of plans can change anytime, I give myself a little wiggle room for sudden schedule movements. Our lives would be too boring if we do it to the dot, wouldn't they? So, keep your daily schedules organized but leave room for impromptu activities and enough breaks to rest.

Apart from our schedules, I also write down all the reminders such as bills to pay, items in the pantry that need to be replenished, and other important appointments. There's also a to-do list on the side so I can keep track of our tasks.

I also maintain a list of things to do on a daily, weekly, monthly, and quarterly basis. I do this segregation so I don't get too overwhelmed with the number of tasks I need to accomplish. This also helps me prioritize which one needs immediate attention and which ones need to be scheduled at a later time because, for example, an allotted budget is required to accomplish the task. These are just examples of organizing your schedule. I highly suggest that you also do your own research. Lay out all the learnings you got from other homemakers and choose the ones that work best for you.

When it comes to creating the notebook itself, I prefer using a large, blank one that I can personalize depending on whose schedule I am trying to plot. Alternatively, you can also use the ones that were already made for a specific task. Or you can just download free templates online that you can easily customize and print anytime.

Here's a sample of my daily plan:

4.00 a.m.: Wake-up and drink warm tea

4.30 a.m.: Check to-do list

5.00 a.m.: Check emails on my phone

5.30 a.m.: Prepare breakfast

7.00 a.m.: Send the kids to school

7.30 a.m.: Grocery time

8.45 a.m.: Freshen up

9.00 a.m.: Start of morning meetings

12 noon: Pick-up kids from school

12.30 p.m.: Lunch

1.00 p.m.: Siesta time (this is very important!)

3.00 p.m.: Start of afternoon meetings

3.30 p.m.: Prepare for merienda

4.30 p.m.: Walking with kids

5.30 p.m.: Start of my online class until 8.30 p.m.

6.30 p.m.: Angels to prepare our dinner

7.30 p.m.: Dinner

8.00 p.m.: Kids' assignment time

9.30 p.m.: Pray and kids' bedtime

10.30 p.m.: Start and check tomorrow's to-do list

And here's one featuring a sample of my weekly meal plan. I cannot NOT include this in the book because I know how much you all love this as it also serves as your own guide for when you become too busy to plan your weekly meals.

MIRANDA'S

MEAL PLAN

MONDAY

BREAKFAST
TOCILOG
LUNCH & DINNER
FRIED CHICKEN
PANCIT
SNACK
GARLIC TOAST PIZZA

TUESDAY

BREAKFAST
DAING
LUNCH & DINNER
ARROZ ALA CUBANA
SNACK
TACOS

WEDNESDAY

BREAKFAST
SCRAMBLED EGGS
LUNCH & DINNER
PINAKBET & FISH
SNACK
FRESH FRUITS

THURSDAY

BREAKFAST
CHAMPORADO
LUNCH & DINNER
PORK STEAK
SNACK
GRILLED CHEESE
SANDWICH

FRIDAY

BREAKFAST
SPAM RICE
LUNCH & DINNER
TINAPA & MUNGGO
SNACK
OATMEAL COOKIES

SATURDAY

BREAKFAST
PANCAKE
LUNCH & DINNER
CHICKEN ADOBO
SNACK
TURON

WAIS TIP #45: GO BARGAIN HUNTING!

From food to furniture to clothes, I love going around cities and finding the best deals for all! Each time I score a good deal, it makes my mommy-heart leap with joy and inspires me to look out for more. I understand that some people might think that when you go bargain hunting it automatically means you are unable to afford expensive items. And that your preference is a reflection of your poor financial status. I get it.

But in this book, I aim to help erase the stigma. This is why, as a Wais Na Misis I want to somehow get it into your system that there is nothing wrong with bargain shopping. In fact, it is one of the top skills that will make you an even better Wais Na Misis.

I promise you, it's among the most enjoyable and exciting ways for you to save money while being able to get the things that you need and want for your home. It's also a good opportunity for you to exercise your creativity and haggling skills. Let me share with you some of my tried and tested tips to get you started:

1. **FOCUS:** What is it that you are trying to accomplish? Are you going bargain-hunting for your new home's kitchen? Or are you into thrift shopping for your vacation clothes?
2. **LIST:** Once you have finalized your goal, write a list of the specific items that you need to help you plan out your shopping day efficiently. Doing this also ensures that you won't miss out on any important item.
3. **BUDGET:** If you don't have one yet, you better set one now! Since this is thrift shopping, going all out on your hard-earned cash defeats the purpose of the activity. Before you head out, make sure you have already decided how much you are willing to spend on each item. This will also help you haggle when you find something that suits your needs. Carry your budget in cash so you can easily track your expenses and check how much you still have left. Resist the urge to use online banking unless needed.
4. **RESEARCH:** Ask around or Google thrift stores, warehouses, and outlet stores around your area and visit the ones nearest to you first to save time. Online secondhand shops like Facebook Marketplace are also good options if you don't have the time and means to go out just yet. Ask for your friends' recommendations or post a question on social media about where to best shop. I'm sure online community will be willing to help!

WAIS TIP #46: CREATE A 'COMMAND CENTER'

First, let me define what a command center is in the Miranda household. It's basically a small spot in our house that's dedicated to all the important things that the family needs to know and they must have access to. It's a lot like a community bulletin board, to put it simply. It can be a blank space in your kitchen, the wall in front or behind your office table, or in our case, our backdoor (check out our video on Youtube titled 'DIY Command Center ft. Chito Miranda').

I chose this part of our house because almost everyone goes into the main kitchen at some point. I also strategically positioned it on the door since it's the main passageway to our laundry area, dirty kitchen, and angels (we call our helpers our angels because they help us maintain our home and they make our lives easier) quarters. Again, everyone goes through it.

Since I am not always around and available to remind everyone about their individual to-do lists, I will just have to post the reminders on the command center so they can check it out anytime they are available. Having a common place, like a command center, can help make an efficient household system because everyone in the family knows where to get what (like bills, receipts, keys, and other knick-knacks). Lastly, this encourages the household to be more responsible. Because if they miss out on any appointment or reminder, they have no one to blame but themselves for not checking the command center for it.

Just so you have an idea (you can always tweak it to fit your lifestyle and household), I have on my command center the following information so we all can keep track of anytime:

- Kids' checkup schedule
- Pets' checkup schedule
- Cars' maintenance schedule
- Bills' due dates
- Meal plans
- Paper bills and letters
- Car and house keys

Now, don't be intimidated okay? If you can check my Youtube video tutorial about it, you'll see how easy it is to assemble your own command center. I have listed below the main items that you'll need to carry the essentials. But, feel free to add more and customize it to your liking. And, as with every project or suggestion that I share with you in this book, DON'T FORGET TO HAVE FUN while doing it!

COMMAND CENTER ESSENTIALS

- Corkboard or whiteboard (Bills, Daily tasks, Meal plans for the week)
- Whiteboard marker
- Magnets
- Baskets (that can hold paper bills, letters, receipts)
- Hooks and wire mesh for keys

WAIS TIP #47: BUILD YOUR OWN VEGETABLE GARDEN

I love gardening, I love everything that has to do with planting flowers, vegetables, or fruits. I grew being exposed to it so it wasn't difficult for me when I decided to start my own backyard vegetable garden in Alfonso. For some of you, gardening is too much of a hassle. It is messy and it is tedious to maintain. I can't blame you, though, because this is the reality of gardening. Even my husband used to see it this way.

What changed was when he was able to personally experience harvesting huge vegetables and other fresh produce using his own hands. We'd consume heaps of tomatoes and calamansi because he loves mixing his own dips and sauces. Imagine his happiness when he realized he could just walk to our backyard garden and pick out the freshest tomatoes and calamansi, in fact, as much as his hands could carry and have them ready to make his special sauce!

The pandemic, though heartbreaking, helped him understand how important it was that we grew our own food. When it had become a challenge for everyone to go outside and buy food from the supermarket, we had little to no problem doing so. All we had to do was take a trip to our garden and harvest whatever vegetable or fruit we needed for our meals without the danger of contracting the dreaded virus.

As for my kids, growing our own vegetables continuously encourages them to eat more of it because they can actually see where the food we serve comes from. To make it even more exciting, I also let them tag along and harvest with me, so they eventually become familiar with the kinds we have and more. I just hope and pray that through their constant exposure to gardening, they will also be inspired to build and maintain one when they grow up.

How about you? Have you thought of starting one? If you haven't then maybe this is your sign! Roll up your sleeves, grab your gardening tools, and let's build your garden! Let me share with you how:

1. **FIND YOUR BEST SPOT:** Choose the area in your backyard that receives the most amount of sunlight. Research, too, on the types of plants, vegetables, and fruits that are best suited to grow with the kind of climate that your location has. Also, don't forget to consider the amount of space you have available because plants don't grow well in a crowded place. There are also vegetables that are sensitive to touch and movement like squash. Mine didn't grow well before because I kept touching and moving it. So, now that I know better, I give my plants some room to grow and I allow them to do so on their own.

2. **CHOOSE WHAT YOU WANT TO PLANT:** Consider the climate, amount of sunlight, and type of soil when you choose the kinds of plants you want to include in your garden. For starters, you can try growing pechay since it is fairly low maintenance and you can harvest it after around two to three months. Based on my experience, vegetables like *mustasa* (mustard greens), okra, cucumber, tomato, and calamansi are the easiest ones to grow.

3. **MAKE SURE TO PREP THE SOIL:** This is one of the most important, if not the most important, step in building the perfect vegetable garden. Using your gardening tools, remove weeds, grass, rocks, and other debris from the area. Try to loosen the soil using a tiller or garden fork and add compost or fertilizer to improve its condition.

4. **MAINTAIN YOUR GARDEN:** Make sure that you water your plants regularly and protect them from pests and insects, too. I like using my own natural insecticide concoction that's made of water and crushed garlic and chili. I don't use the ones that are synthetic or chemical-based because it is obviously harmful to plants as well as to humans.

    Building your own vegetable garden requires a lot of effort and patience but the benefits are super worth it. Just take it slow and enjoy the process.

Chapter 15

Dear Ate Neri

I get quite a lot of questions within and outside my social media accounts. Most of them are about loyalty in a relationship and other similar concerns. Sometimes, the questions would jump from self-improvement and creating better relationships, to home hacks, and other random stuff. I would answer these questions, post them on my Instagram page, and put them in one Instagram highlight tab called *Dear Ate Neri* so everyone can read it anytime. If the questions were either asked in person or would require longer explanations, I would answer and post them on my Youtube channel.

Having said that, there were questions that I found interesting and I thought of sharing them with you in this book. But since some, if not all, of them may not fit into any of the chapters, I have decided to dedicate one for them instead.

So, with this, I sincerely thank everyone who has trusted me with their personal problems. It is a privilege and a huge honour to be able to help you in my own little way. Thank you for considering my advice, guidance, and wisdom. Thank you for choosing me to help you navigate through the important seasons and decisions of your life.

All the hardships and challenges that I have experienced from childhood until today are serving their purpose. And with this, I pray for more opportunities to be able to serve you, my fellow Wais Na Misis.

(NOTE: Questions have been edited for clarity and anonymity)

Q: CAN YOU SHARE SOME TIPS FOR BECOMING A WIFE WITHOUT LOSING YOURSELF?

A: Being a wife doesn't mean you need to give up on your personal goals and ambitions. In fact, a supportive spouse (like Chito!) will encourage and support you in achieving your dreams and will help you become the best version of yourself even when your new priorities are each other and your family. Don't forget to pursue and enjoy the hobbies and the things that you used to do even before you got married.

Whether it's painting, dancing, singing, or as crazy as bungee jumping, not giving up what you love doing will help you maintain your personality and sense of self.

Q: WHAT IF YOUR MOTHER-IN-LAW DOESN'T LIKE YOU? WHAT DO YOU DO?

A: Continue being a good mom, wife, and person in general. If she still doesn't like you despite your good attitude and disposition then you are not the problem. As long as she doesn't physically hurt you, you can always ignore her and turn your focus on your family and yourself. You can also consider sharing this problem with your husband so you can work on it together. After all, you are each other's allies.

Q: HOW DO YOU HANDLE YOUR ANGER WHEN YOU THOUGHT YOUR HUSBAND'S FRIEND WAS JUST VISITING BUT THEY DON'T TELL YOU THAT THEY ACTUALLY HAVE PLANS TO GO OUT THAT DAY? I WANT TO BURST IN ANGER BUT I AM TRYING TO CONTROL IT BECAUSE I DON'T WANT TO HUMILIATE HIM IN FRONT OF HIS FRIEND. HELP!

A: This hasn't happened to me yet but, for the sake of trying to provide an answer to your concern, all I can say is that Chito and I have already established the kind of relationship where he doesn't need to hide anything from me. Maybe you can begin on that with your spouse?

If Chito wants to go out with our or his friends without me, I'm okay with it because I am such a homebody that staying behind is as good for me as going out. All I can say is that whatever your issue is with your husband, try not to be angry. Being so prevents you both from being able to deal with the real issue at hand. Anger can also lead to unnecessary arguments that might ruin your relationship in the process. Don't allow the anger to get the best of you. Let your husband and his friend go out without you and just talk to your husband about his attitude and decisions later when he gets back home.

Talk calmly and speak nicely.

Q: HOW CAN I BALANCE BEING A MOM WHILE PURSUING MY CAREER OR PERSONAL GOALS?

A: Like what I've always said, you have to have a to-do list that you prepare the night before. At the end of the day try to assess everything that you have done throughout the day. Having this helps you balance your personal and professional life and for me seeing the proof on paper helps a lot. You'll see here how well you distribute your time for both and you can think of a solution right away.

Q: HOW DO I DISCIPLINE MY CHILD WITHOUT BEING TOO HARSH OR TOO LENIENT?

A: I grew up in a home where the adults don't like explaining anything. They command me to do something without telling me why I have to do it or why a certain thing needs to happen. It was a one-way communication and it left me confused as I grew up. So now, with my kids whenever I ask them to do anything or reprimand them for something that they did, I make sure to let them know that I am not mad at them and that I am just trying to make them do it for some other reasons. I also make sure that I do it with a gentle tone (not baby talk!) but with authority that I am still their mom as I explain things to them. I do my best for them to understand why a certain move needs to be made and what are the effects of doing it. Our kids, your kids, are smart little human beings, don't underestimate their understanding. Talk to them like adults and explain to them what it is that they need to understand. I do this because I don't want them to grow up being scared of me or seeing me as someone whom they cannot go to when they mess up because in their heads I will probably scold them.

Q: PLEASE HELP ME. I HAVE BEEN HAVING FEELINGS OF GUILT AND INADEQUACY AS A MOTHER. HOW DO I DEAL WITH THESE?

A: There are days, too, when I feel like I am such a failure. I think most moms feel this way and let me tell you that it's okay to feel that way. What I do is acknowledge my feelings. I don't deny it otherwise I may not be able to do something about it. Then I pause for a bit and think of the things that I have been doing. If there are things that I might have missed out on doing for my family or if I wasn't able to do a few things from my personal to-do lists, I try to be gentle on myself and tell myself that it's okay if I wasn't able to accomplish any of it for now, there is still another day to do it. If I feel like I did something wrong, I analyse it. If it's fixable, then I try to do something about it.

Otherwise, I will just let it go. Be kind to yourself. There's only one of you.

I also avoid comparing myself to other moms. I'm the type of person who admires another instead of comparing myself to them. Because I know that we moms are all doing our best for our families. So there's no use getting envious or comparing myself to how other moms take on their roles. Always remember that you are enough.

PART 4: Stronger, Better, WAIS-er!

Chapter 16

Saved to Serve

Remember my brush with death story? Let me refresh your memory. It's the one where I was trying to gather as much kaning baboy as I possibly could for the day. I had to cross the highway to get to the other side of the neighbourhood. When I was about halfway through the highway, I was almost swiped by a speeding provincial bus. I seriously believe that the angel assigned to me that day must have pulled me back in the nick of time so I wouldn't get hit. If I had not taken a tiny step back, I'd have collided with the bus. Or better yet, God saved me that day; no one can convince me otherwise.

I used to ask God, through my diary, why did He allow me to live if I'd only be slapped by my mom? Why did He wake me up so I could go to school and be bullied over and over again? Why did He create me and put me in a family where the dad was often absent and the mom was angry? A few years and a thousand realizations and proofs after the mind-numbing bus incident, I guess I'd finally gotten my answer. Perhaps, I was saved to serve Him because He didn't just bless me with another day to live. He gave me thirty plus more years and a heart that is just full of desire to do something, big or small, for a fellow human since that day.

Because of this, I saw life from a different perspective. I knew it wasn't just about me any more. Knowing that I have a purpose, be it to serve my husband, my kids, the rest of my family, or the community around me, makes me want to become a better person every day. After all, how can I serve others if I am not at my best?

Making the conscious decision to serve has done a great deal of improvement in my day-to-day living, especially now that I am a mom. It has also helped me become a better entrepreneur because I don't see a business as merely a tool to get more money just for myself. It has now evolved into an opportunity to help make other people's lives become better, with the hope of passing on the same opportunities to others until the blessing freely flows down to the next generations.

Because I know what I was meant to do in this world (If you still don't, be patient. Pray about it and ask God to help you find it or ask Him to show you!), I am conscious about the kinds of decisions I now make. My simple 'YES' or 'NO' can create a big difference in the outcome. It can bring me closer to my goal, take me farther away from it, or totally lead me astray.

But, if you think you are having a hard time finding your ultimate purpose, go easy on yourself and enjoy living one day at a time. It will come to you at the right moment. In the meantime, why not try and intentionally become a Wais Na Misis (or Wais Na Human Being in general hehe) while you are still trying to figure out your purpose?

Whatever you'll get out of the last chapters of this book is all yours to use whatever way you want to. Just take it. It's better to have it and not need it than need it and not have it.

Get it? Awesome.

Now, are you ready to become even stronger, better, and Waiser? Let's go!

WAIS TIP #48: YOUR DECISIONS SHOULD BRING YOU CLOSER TO YOUR GOALS

I always tell people who ask me for life advice that the choice they make should lead them to the path that's carved for their dreams.

Be intentional.

Knowing who I wanted to be in this life (a mom!), where I want to go and spend most of my days (on the farm!), and what I want to achieve (a better life for my family) have made my life so much easier. This kind of technique has helped me narrow down my choices and decide confidently for of the kind of outcome I am looking forward to.

Let's say, for example, I want to bake a cake. Before I would even step into the supermarket, I already know that I will head straight to the baking essentials where the flour, baking powder, sugar, and the rest of the related ingredients are kept. Because my goal is to make a cake, I will not linger in the frozen food section or spend much time in the canned goods aisle unless one of the cake ingredients can be found there. I'll simply head straight to where the main items are, gather everything I need, head to the cashier, pay, and leave. As simple as that. I could have checked out other items and shopped for my pantry but it will have definitely eaten up my day, leaving me with lesser to no time for the cake I wanted to bake.

The point here is that starting today, be mindful of every decision you make. Okay, so just to give you an idea, every time I'm faced with making one, I always ask myself either of these: 'Will this benefit my family or my businesses?', 'Will my response make me a better person or will I just be serving my ego?', or 'If my kids see what I have done, is this something that they can be proud of? Is it something worth copying?'

Having these in mind saves me from the irreversible consequences of my rash actions. I remember one time when Chito and I just had an argument during our married life.

While he was trying to explain his side of the story, I didn't speak a word the entire time. This pushed Chito to say more and more things just to get me to talk and probably discuss the issue while it was still fresh. I admit, there were statements that might have triggered me had I not chosen silence in the heat of the moment.

So, instead of giving in to the argument, I left the scene, took a shower, and calmed myself down. It wasn't long enough before I heard Chito by the room shower area and still talking about the same agenda. I am trying to stop myself from laughing as I type this because I remember hearing him right outside the door and trying to get a word out of me. Instead, I kept on shampooing my hair (I must have done it five times!) just to stop myself from getting into an argument with him. I mean, what for? If we got into a heated discussion at the moment, we'd definitely have said hurtful things that we didn't mean and worse, it would have cost us our relationship.

My goal then was to keep our relationship thriving and surviving. And not talking back or responding while I was angry or filled with negative emotions. This was a conscious decision that obviously led me to where we are now. Had I done otherwise, there might not even be a Pamilya Miranda today.

WAIS TIP #49: YOUR RESPONSE TO ANY SITUATION CAN HELP SHAPE THE LIVES OF THE PEOPLE AROUND YOU

We all want to be treated nicely and with respect. No one wants to be seen as anything lower than a human being. Am I right? This is why I have included this Wais tip to remind you that as a Wais person, you now have to be mindful of your actions because people are watching and some of them even look up to you (most especially your kids!). Not that we should care all the time and have their opinions run our lives, but because we all have our own spheres of influence that, whether we like it or not, will definitely be affected by how we handle things.

Take, for example, my mom and her way of handling her emotions. She sure must have been greatly influenced by the kind of environment and the way people have treated her in the past for her to become the aggressive and ill-tempered person toward me when I was growing up. I will not say that I was okay because I wasn't. I may be carrying its negative effects up to this day, who knows? I just am thankful for God's grace that He gave me a new and fresh way of seeing things and protected me from turning into a harmful person because of what she did. Because of our past, I am now careful about how I act in front of my family. I do my best not to repeat what has happened to me and my mom before.

I have experienced how to be treated with so much anger by my mom when I was just asking an innocent question. And I have seen and understood the ugly effects of bickering, shouting, and physically hurting each other from how my parents handled their issues as a couple. I could've turned into an awful person or I could've just easily been a replica of my mom if I didn't grasp early on this life-changing idea stated in this Wais tip. I could've simply recreated my childhood life, this time in a bigger house and with access to more resources, and could have passed on the trauma to my family because I didn't know any better. So, I am passing this reminder on to you.

And if you find yourself in a situation where you don't know how to best respond, always choose to take the route of kindness. It sounds cliché but it is the best choice.

WAIS TIP #50: ALWAYS CHOOSE TO BE KIND. BUT, DON'T BE A PUSHOVER!

Being kind becomes easier for us each time we do it. The more we do it, the more we become better at it. Whenever I don't know how to act in a certain situation, I just choose to be kind. I don't fight back, I just walk away and assert my boundaries by doing so. When I feel triggered, I am always reminded of the times that I have been saved from a terrible or humiliating situation because I did not retaliate and I chose to be kind. Plus, I sleep soundly like a baby at night because I chose kindness over getting my way, proving my point, or shoving my worth down people's throats.

Let me share with you a story that happened way way back when I was a fairly young actress and a bit more active in show business. I remember one time, I was fresh out of Star Circle Quest. We were filming a Christmas special for a TV network. Since it's the holidays and, green and red were symbolic colours of the season, I wore my thrifted, green A-line skirt that's accented with small red roses all over it. I felt like Audrey Hepburn or Grace Kelly wearing the 30-pesos skirt as it sure made me feel so pretty.

However, someone from the set who was with me filming the Christmas special thought otherwise. I didn't bother checking out who he or she was. All I remember was the nasty comment got picked up by the microphone on the set and I heard it when I passed them by. The voice said: *'Ano ba 'yan, ang pangit. Ang baduy. Parang pinabili lang ng suka 'to.'* (She looks ugly and uncool. It's as if she was just asked to buy vinegar from the store.) In short, I looked like I probably didn't dress well, was unprepared, and a little too casual based on their standards, when for me, I was already at my prettiest. I also heard them eventually laugh at me right after saying the hurtful comment.

Shocked and definitely offended, I looked at one of the staff with pleading eyes, almost as if I was asking what to do. The staff, who heard it, responded as if to comfort me: *'Wag mo na silang pansinin.'* (Don't mind them.) in a calm yet professional manner. I nodded and focused on the task at hand, which was to perform well for a Christmas special. During the entire taping day, I tried to be unbothered on the outside. But, in reality, I wanted to cry my heart out because, let's face it, their comment about my clothes was hurtful. It was a toss between crying or moving on, to be honest with you. I just tried to remind myself by saying: *'Okay, Neri, nangyari na 'to dati nung bata ka. Alam mo na dapat ang gagawin mo.'* (Okay, Neri, the same thing happened when you were younger. You should know what to do.) Trusting my own reminder and what the staff had said to me, I took a deep breath, stood straight, pulled my shoulders back, and tried my best to focus on the show's director's instructions. The shoot went well, and I went home with a clear conscience.

Yet again, my character had been put to the test. During the filming of a *teleserye*, I was the subject of ridicule but this time by a staff member. At first, I didn't know why she was annoyed at me, but later on, I found out that she had a huge crush on one actor who was secretly courting me. The staff must've figured it out thus the constant bullying during the entire duration of the show. That staff would sometimes team up with other members of the staff to make me feel bad during tapings because of the same reason. There would be days when the production assistant would not help me find the next set location out of spite. It sometimes would take another kind co-actor to tell them to bring me to the next location before they would do it.

One of the worst, if not the worst, bullying I've ever had to experience on the same project was when I was already changing from my character's clothes into my normal ones inside a restroom that was too far from where we were shooting. We were getting ready to leave when a production assistant approached us and told us that I shouldn't change my clothes yet because I was still needed for a scene.

We needed to retake it for safety. In hindsight, I remember the production assistant trying to stifle her laugh while she was saying those things. I should've taken it as a sign. But, anyway, I told Ninang Mace, who started as my personal assistant that time, that it was a good thing that I hadn't removed my hair and makeup yet so I could just easily slip into my character's clothes. After prepping for the retake, we went to the set on foot despite the distance. We got there huffing and puffing like we had just ran a marathon, but we didn't see any active scene. In fact, there was no set at all! The entire production had already packed up and left. And apparently, the same staff who hated me because the actor she liked was interested in me, along with the production assistant, had played a hurtful prank on me. She probably wanted to make my life even more difficult than it was for whatever reason she had at that time.

It sure made me and Ninang Mace mad. I was played with and I was deeply hurt. It was a convenient reason for me to just give up and quit acting. But, I had dreams. I was already in show business and I wanted to earn more for my family so I did my best while I was in it. I grieved over what had happened but I didn't allow it to get the best of me.

And, oh! One last story. This might be a lengthy one but bear with me. It's a good story, I promise you!

One time, we were shooting the same *teleserye* at another location where the owner of the house we were filming in was a friend of my college friend. So naturally, my college friend had told her friend, the owner, about it. The owner expressed her desire to meet me, because of our common friend, and so I was informed that they will drop by the next taping day.

When I learned that the owner had arrived, I immediately looked for her and introduced myself. Even if we didn't have a common friend, I'd really have gone out of my way to even say 'Hi! because that's basic courtesy regardless of anything.

I was surprised when, during the short chat we had, the homeowner gave me one room in her mansion so I could privately rest, she said. Actors are usually placed in a common holding area where we can eat, nap, and wait before our scene. Sometimes, too, it would be an added production cost if everyone got their own rooms so only the bigger stars are given a private room with a toilet probably because they need longer rests, they have more stuff to bring, and well, they've basically earned every right to have one.

So, anyway, the homeowner offered me my own room because I was her friend's friend and so I could have more room to take naps since the assigned holding area was too crowded. I initially refused because I didn't want to look like a primadonna but she insisted. I didn't have the heart to say no to a common friend and a private room to take breaks in. Eventually, I took the offer and settled in.

When the production assistant saw that I was staying in a room all for myself, she barged in and harshly told me that I wasn't supposed to have a room. She even posted a sign outside the common holding area that said: '*DITO LANG ANG WAITING AREA NG MGA ARTISTA, PWERA LANG SA MGA SENYORA. ANO, SIKAT KA?!*' (THIS IS THE ONLY WAITING AREA FOR ACTORS, EXCEPT FOR THE SENIOR ONES. ARE YOU THAT FAMOUS?!)

I left the room and went back to the common holding area where everyone was. But, the homeowner might have probably become a little too fond of me as she kept telling me to take the room again and not to worry about it. I really didn't want to cause any more trouble so I kept on refusing. I eventually gave in when, during one break, the homeowner called again for me to be in the room she was offering me. Unfortunately, a staff saw me go into the room after being told to vacate it. Without any knowledge about what had happened on a parallel side, the staff angrily reprimanded me and told me I had no right to request my own room at all costs. Thank goodness, the homeowner was still around and heard what had just happened. She approached us and told the staff that it was her idea that she wanted me to have a room.

She also must've seen the puzzled look on the staff's face because she quickly introduced herself as the owner of the mansion and my friend. This caught the staff off guard so she just left and let me be.

I thought the worst was over but after that, I experienced even more bullying during the taping. As mentioned in the previous chapter, the situation had gotten so bad that I called my handler to tell our big boss to just kill my character in the show. I had been constantly bullied for days, it wasn't healthy any more, and I just wanted my character dead so I could leave the show.

The staff must have heard it through the lapel mic or they might have been reprimanded by the higher-ups, or better yet, the homeowner (who resembles a dear old aunt filled with wisdom and authority) might have given them a little warning because when I went down to the holding area, they were now all so nice to me.

The point here is that even when it was hard to choose to be the better person, I did my best to do it because I really believe that God sees everything. He is going to do the avenging, not me. So, I chose the kindness route but I didn't allow them to continue treating me badly. Because kindness, for me, goes hand in hand with not being a pushover.

I did not retaliate but I also did not allow them to treat me badly again by being a professional on set; by politely saying NO to things that do not make me feel safe and comfortable; and by using my common sense to leave the situation in which my mental health will suffer.

Be kind but don't forget to set your boundaries.

WAIS TIP #51: FOCUS ON IMPROVING YOURSELF, THAT'S THE BEST REVENGE

In order for me to serve God and become the best mom, wife, daughter, friend, and business partner, I am always on the lookout for opportunities to improve myself. This has also been my mindset, not only when I feel that I am lacking in something but when I'd be wronged. I guess I just am not the kind of person to plot revenge. It didn't come as easy as dreaming of the next investment or business venture to achieve.

God must have programmed me differently. When I was younger, whenever I'd be the a victim of bullying because of my looks, financial status, or the way I think; my initial plan of action would be to work on what's good about me at the moment so my ugly parts wouldn't be highlighted, instead of clapping back or getting into fights to defend myself. For example, I wasn't book-smart in school but I knew I enjoyed being a girl scout, and I did what I could to become better at it. I may not be the smartest one in the class but I sure could be of great help when it comes to surviving outdoors. This resulted in me having new and better sets of friends and less time to even think about the bullies because I was busy with my tribe.

This mindset has helped me deal with the people who used to say bad things about me when I got together with Chito. They'd even tell Chito that I was just pretending to be nice; that I was just using Chito for clout because he is the famous frontman of Parokya Ni Edgar and I was just an actress who didn't reach fame during her time. By this time, you know how I don't respond to triggers easily so yep, you guessed it! I ignored them and continued to live my life. I even helped Chito grow his money while I was consistently improving myself and taking classes. Because of my non-response to their pathetic efforts and lies to bring me down, eventually, one person who used to think bad about me approached me and apologized after Chito and I got married.

One person even told me she thought I was really mean because that was what she heard from her friend and she blindly believed it. 'Yes, I know. I am even aware of the names you were calling me,' I replied. *'Bakit 'di mo kami kinonfront about it?'* (Why didn't you confront us about it?) the girl asked. So I politely responded, *'Di ko kayo kailangan isa-isahin d'yan kasi hindi naman kayo nag-mamatter.'* (I don't need to deal with you individually for that because you don't matter.)

With that, I simply smiled and turned away.

My fellow Wais Na human beings, I know it is hard not to be angry or seek revenge. But, remember you can't fight fire with fire. When you are wronged, be smart enough to know when to speak up and when to stay silent. When to stand your ground and when to walk away. If the need to retaliate appears, pray and do your best to channel your energy into something that your future self will thank you for. You'll sleep better at night, too.

Chapter 17

The World Is My Classroom

I was born with a huge disadvantage, by the world's standards. There were a lot of things that I wasn't able to experience at certain seasons in my life because I lacked the resources, one of which was money. But, I didn't allow it to hold me back. I didn't let it keep me from winning and enjoying life. Instead, I used them as stepping stones and motivations to work harder and smarter so I can have a better one moving forward.

Because I know that if I get the chance to have it, then my future family will eventually, too.

When I could no longer change the situation; when I could not rewind my life and choose the elements, I learned to make the most out of my present no matter how silly I may appear to others.

I've been asked one too many times about the secret to becoming a Wais Na Misis. To tell you honestly, what I do is not a secret at all. In fact, it's something that anyone, even if you're not a *misis,* can do.

I never stopped learning.

Our natural tendency is to be contented when we have reached the expert level. We stop at the sign of success and we become complacent when we feel like we have known enough. On the contrary, we also tend to shrink when we feel like we don't know anything. And sometimes, we even feel ashamed when our ignorance is exposed.

Where do we stand? How do we overcome this?

WAIS TIP #52: DON'T BE AFRAID TO COMMIT MISTAKES AND LEARN FROM IT

It all boils down to ego. There, I had to say it. Our ego sometimes prevents us from improving because it instantly turns a learning opportunity into an offense that's a little too personal. This, in turn, discourages us to push forward despite it. Okay, allow me to illustrate this part by sharing with you another story.

I was around twenty-one or twenty-two when I went out with my ex-boyfriend this one time to have lunch. We had *sinigang,* a sour soup-based pork dish, and I've loved that dish since childhood, so imagine my excitement at the table. Feeling happy and hungry, I casually poured the broth from the main bowl onto my bowl the way I used to back in Subic and Baguio. For me, it was the most normal thing to do because that was what I had been doing all my life until then.

When I saw the people at the table around me slowly stop what they were doing and awkwardly staring at me for a good minute, I knew I was doing something wrong. As someone who grew up in the province with no concept of proper table etiquettes, I didn't know at that time that a serving spoon was supposed to be used to transfer the food from the main dish to our bowls. I wasn't raised a caveman, just to be clear. But because I grew up with little to no exposure to the cultural norms and no one in my family took the time to teach me the ropes, I literally had no clue about it.

It was a pretty humiliating experience to be around people and mess up on something that even a toddler knows. My ex-boyfriend even had to make a disclaimer that I shouldn't be judged too soon because I haven't gotten any training on table etiquette. If a helicopter with a hanging ladder appeared out of nowhere or the ground had opened up to serve as an escape route, I'd have immediately taken the chance. No ifs and buts. I just wanted to disappear.

But, you know me, I was and still am a fighter. After that incident, I immediately browsed the internet for local schools that offered classes on basic etiquettes, proper decorum, and building personal image. Thankfully I found one and quickly enrolled. Furthermore, I started to carefully read newspapers and ensure that I was updated with the latest news, not just in the Philippines, but all over the world. I wanted to contribute with my knowledge to the conversations happening around, should I find myself in one, most especially with people at work.

If you mess up, which we all do at some point in our lives because we are merely humans, you will always have a choice. It's either you let the mistake or that humiliating experience eat you alive or you take it by its horns and use it to your advantage. A mistake, especially a public one, is going to hurt your feelings and your ego. But, you don't have to let one moment define your entire existence. With all the remaining strength that you have, stand up, dust yourself off, slowly walk away, and come back stronger. How? By consistently improving yourself.

Now, how does one exactly do this, you may ask? Let me walk you through some of the steps I used to take, instead of wallowing in self-pity, that helped me become better:

1. **ACKNOWLEDGE:** I do not deny the incident. I do my best to admit that it happened and that I have committed a mistake. By recognizing and taking ownership of the situation I am also avoiding making excuses and putting the blame on others.
2. **ANALYSE:** As soon as I get home, I try to remember every detail possible about the incident. Then I try to identify what went wrong and what could be the possible points for improvement. This helps me become aware of the situation and it helps me avoid making the same mistakes in the future.
3. **LEARN:** Once I have a thorough assessment of the situation, I run through each mistake and I try to think of how I can avoid it next time. I would usually come up with a plan like enrolling in a class, talking to a friend who is an expert on the subject matter, or reading books about it.
4. **ACT:** The moment I have decided on a solution, I don't take long before making a move. I act on it before my mind comes up with a hundred ways for me not to do it. Sometimes, it helps if I share my plan with a trusted friend or tell it to Chito because I am now accountable and responsible for what I have just said. It helps me become more committed to the plan and the chances of backing out of it become smaller and smaller.

5. **BREATHE:** In the process of trying to improve myself, I also recognize the fact that along the way I will unintentionally commit different mistakes. With this realization, I go easy on myself. I practice self-compassion because mistakes are as normal as breathing. We are humans after all. I try not to beat myself up over something that I couldn't get at first go. Instead, I shift my focus on how my body usually responds to the changes and use it to my advantage so I can grasp whatever it is I'm trying to learn easily.

WAIS TIP #53: YOU DON'T NEED TO SPEND SO MUCH MONEY TO LEARN SOMETHING NEW

Okay, I know nothing is free in this life, most especially in this day and age. But, hear me out okay? When I say go out there and improve on yourself, take classes, and learn from the world, I am not saying you go and spend your hard-earned money all the time.

I came from nothing. And what I learned is that there are as many free lessons out there as there are paid. You just have to be hungry enough to search for them and grab them. But anyway, to get you started, here are some of the places where I've gotten most of my FREE training and lessons from. If you're still a bit clueless, you can start from any among the list:

ONLINE SCHOOLS: Not a single soul hasn't gotten online learning in this era. coursera.org and edX.org have some of the best free online classes there are. From computer programming to marketing, and even makeup artistry. Name it and they probably have it.

Just note that there are some courses that require fees if you want to have a diploma-certificate or a completion-certificate sent to you.

BRAND PROMOTIONS: If you have a favourite brand, watch out for their monthly activities because oftentimes, they hold free workshops or classes to support and push for their product promotions.

APPRENTICESHIP & SCHOLARSHIP PROGRAMMES: There are generous brands, companies, and individual experts out there with big big hearts who occasionally open their calendars for apprenticeship programmes. This is your chance! Make sure to fill up any questionnaire or attempt exams diligently and follow the application instructions well.

YOUTUBE: This has got to be the world's most-attended online university. In fact, many experts have gotten their masters here. Nah, I'm just kidding. But, beyond the entertaining videos lie the hidden gems of this platform. A lot of experts and brands have been using this for a long time now to share their knowledge mainly because they want to or because it's in partnership with an establishment or a brand. Either way, it provides users free information that was only usually found in school. Just be careful of the kind of information that you absorb since everyone can use it and have access to it. Not everything's reliable so it's better cross-check it with other resources.

CLOSE FRIENDS OR RELATIVES: You might have an aunt who is successful in her chosen field, so maybe try to schedule an afternoon with her to pick her brain. Or how about a friend who has a masters in the same subject you are interested in? Ask for a quick catch-up and for sure, you'll learn a lot in no time. A follow-up session might even be needed and prove helpful. Don't be too shy to ask your friends for help. They're more than happy to share with you what they know. Just make sure your schedules align and that you treat them to a meal or two after!

Chapter 18

Imperfect Love

I have had a lot of love-and-hate moments with myself. But, more often than not, I find myself trying to love myself more, especially on days when people and circumstances make it difficult to do so. Because I grew up receiving so much hate and anger from people from different seasons in my life, I have now become naturally inclined to become my own best friend.

Maybe this has been a part of God's design for my life, to love myself enough, so I can eventually help others love themselves, no matter how we all sometimes feel inadequate and imperfect. Loving myself wasn't always an easy task but I do my best to do it as it has become one of the most important aspects of my being a Wais Na Misis. After all, I cannot pour from an empty cup and I cannot give what I do not have.

During my forty years of existence, I have slowly learned that self-love is not just about setting healthy boundaries and loving the ideal and Instagram-able parts of me. I mean, those are easy c'mon! But self-love is also about accepting myself, split ends, cracked heels, stretch marks, and all. This kind of love, though imperfect because I still find myself unlovable at times, has also taught me to be more forgiving and less critical of myself. Now, there's more freedom than pressure, I realized, and compassion than comparison. And because I have learned how to fill my own cup, serving the people whom God has assigned me to serve has eventually become as easy as breathing.

You know what? I can talk about it for hours but this book wouldn't be enough. So, I'll just share with you some tips on how

I was able to somehow grasp the entire concept of self-love if you are still unsure how and where to begin. Don't worry, it tends to be a little vague at times.

Also, I acknowledge that we are all coming from different backgrounds and pasts. So it is understandable that for some of you, self-love may be an easy thing to do. While for others, it can be the most challenging change that you will have to go through at this point in your life, and that's okay.

Wherever you are at in your life, know that there is no strict timeline for this. There are also no right or wrong decisions. You will only win or you will learn. Go easy on yourself, okay? Take it one day at a time.

Loving yourself can transform your life in countless positive ways. So, how about kicking it off with …

WAIS TIP #54: BE KIND TO YOURSELF

There is only one Neri Naig-Miranda in this vast universe, so I simply chill and try to become a little kinder to myself. Because if I don't, one day I might just crash and burn. So, I give the same kindness and compassion that I would usually extend to my best friend, husband, children, or anyone in general. Whenever I make a mistake or fall short of my expectations on let's say a task or a business project, I briefly acknowledge the shortcomings and I focus on giving myself words of encouragement and support instead of criticism. I often tell myself, 'It's okay, Neri. Breathe. Tomorrow's another day. It's okay.'

If I find myself in high-pressure situations, I take deep but frequent breaths to calm myself down and I hug myself for a little while. Doing this helps me calm my nerves and regain my focus.

WAIS TIP #55: CELEBRATE YOUR UPS AND GRIEVE OVER YOUR LOWS

Another way of being kind to myself is allowing myself to celebrate my best days and grieve over my worst ones. I don't push myself to pretend to be happy all the time when I feel down and I don't feel guilty about rejoicing or rewarding myself when good things come my way. I welcome all emotions as they come and sit with them for a time until they decide it's time to go.

I remember the day when I found out I lost our first baby because of a miscarriage back in 2015. I broke down as soon as I got in our car on our way back from the hospital. I was crying my heart out but it had no sound. It was that terrible of an experience.

When we got home, we even had to meet Chito's family because they had been waiting for us to share the good news. Though I didn't tell them what had happened because I didn't have the strength to do so, I also didn't force myself to look okay and pretend as if nothing heartbreaking had taken place in the last few hours. I was simply tired and devastated, and I allowed myself to feel that.

I was also in the middle of a *teleserye* taping when it happened. But, instead of forcing myself to suck it up and work as if nothing had happened, I told the project head about the miscarriage and that I didn't want to go to work yet because of it. I allow myself to feel bad. I embrace the pain. But, to begin the process of healing, I ask myself if it is still worth it to stay in that state or if it's now time to move forward and do something about it.

You won't see me post a lot of sad stories on my social media accounts but in private, I grieve when sad or hurtful things happen. However, when good things happen like my partners and I were able to open another business, Miggy did a great job with his new painting or his penmanship improved, Ate Pia did another amazing digital artwork, or better yet, Cash finished a plateful of noodles, I instantly post about these with pride. It may look like I am bragging but in reality, that is just my way of celebrating the grace and blessings that have been given to me. I try to immortalize happy memories through my posts so I can use them as inspiration to keep moving forward. I allow myself the time and space to grieve over my bad days so I can use them as opportunities for growth and learning.

WAIS TIP #56: PAMPER YOURSELF ONCE IN A WHILE

My dear Wais Na Misis, you have been working hard for your family. You have been spending more hours hustling and grinding to give your loved ones a better shot at life. You have been giving your 100 per cent to achieve your lifelong dream. Now, take this as a sign and take a break.

What makes you feel relaxed? What sparks your joy? What makes your eyes sparkle with delight? What resets your tired mind?

Any answer that pops into your head (just the safe and legal ones, okay?!) do it! Treat yourself to a much-needed pampering session so you don't burn out quickly. It can be as simple as indulging in extra nap hours or going to the salon (ExtraordiNERI salon ehem …) to get your hair cut. You can even have your hair shampooed and your scalp massaged. Anything that will take your mind off from work and make you feel better at the same time, do it.

I love going to the spa. I love love love getting three-hour body scrubs partnered with a deep and soothing whole body massage. I can say that this is one of the few luxuries (apart from investing in land and properties) I give myself. In fact, I even travel all the way to Metro Manila from Alfonso just to have it done because that's where my favourite spa is.

If you're on a budget, there are a lot of DIY home spa kits or you can search online for instructions on how to set up your personal pamper station at the comfort of your home.

WAIS TIP #57: ALLOW YOURSELF TO BELIEVE THE GOOD THINGS PEOPLE SAY ABOUT YOU

When people say nice things about us, we either shy away from acknowledging it by saying 'Thank you' or we turn it down and tell the person complimenting us that what he or she is saying may not be true. In other words, we don't accept it for fear of looking too full of ourselves or being conceited.

There is a thin line between being modest and false humility when it comes to that, so we turn away from it just to be on the safe side of society. But you know what, if no one has told you yet then let me tell you now: I don't see anything wrong when you accept a compliment and actually believe it. They may or may not mean it but who cares? If it makes you feel better and if it helps you become a better person, take it. Just don't let it get to your head and please don't forget to thank the person who gave you the compliment, okay?

On rare occasions when I feel bad or my spirits are low, I intentionally ask Chito about the things that he loves about me. Because sometimes, I tend to be too overpowered by the negativity and hormonal changes (you girls know this!) that I forget that there is still something lovable or admirable about me. I know, it sounds bordering narcissistic but hey, it helps uplift my mood so why not do it, right? Friendly reminder: I don't ask this question to just about anyone so don't get any ideas. I only ask Chito because he is someone I trust. I know he will tell me everything I need to know with all sincerity and honesty.

Chapter 19

Inner Beauty

'For attractive lips, speak words of kindness. For lovely eyes,
seek out the good in people.
For a slim figure, share your food with the hungry.
For beautiful hair, let a child run his fingers through it once a day.
For poise, walk with the knowledge you'll never walk alone.'
—SAM LEVINSON, In One Era & Out The Other

This chapter naturally follows the one that talks about loving and taking care of yourself. Because once you do, you will realize that the love you give yourself is reflected in how you treat the people around you. YOU BECOME YOUR MOST BEAUTIFUL SELF.

You are not a critic any more but the one who gives the sincerest compliments. You are not remembered for your sarcastic jokes but for your comforting words. You no longer see the glass half empty but always full and overflowing.

Because you have learned to love yourself well, you are now able to love others better. You have become beautiful in your own special way. And in any case, you may have forgotten how beautiful you are, please allow me to remind you that …

WAIS TIP #58: BEAUTIFUL PEOPLE DO NOT SEEK REVENGE

I've endured so many taunts and bullying in the past. I have been called names. I have been accused of being someone I am entirely not. I have been lied to and swindled, too. All of these, by the world's standards, merit revenge. The oppressors need to pay for the bad things that they have done to me so I can get justice. But, my question is, by whose standards? I only reserve the long arm of the law for grave offenses but for the abovementioned ones, I leave them all to our good Lord.

As much as my human tendencies sometimes push me to fight back, the better side of myself pulls me and tells me otherwise. I don't have any rational and logical explanation for why I feel that way. I just know that seeking revenge isn't something that I enjoy doing. Because I truly believe that whatever people do to you, especially the bad ones, says a lot more about them than about you.

When people do me wrong, I take a deep breath and shift my focus to whatever brings me joy. I take the high road, to put it simply. If I can't ignore it entirely, I make myself busy. Instead of giving the offence a headspace, I channel my energy into improving myself. This way, from whichever angle I look at it, I will always emerge the winner.

WAIS TIP #59: BEAUTIFUL PEOPLE SPEAK WORDS THAT BRING LIFE

I was once told that I had no future; that at eighteen years old, I will be pregnant with no husband; that I will be alone all my pathetic life. I was also often regarded as the 'bad luck' when my mom would lose when she gambled. I had been called ugly one too many times that at one point, I'd almost started to believe it.

These words were spoken about me during my younger years. If God hadn't given me the strength to rebuke and believe otherwise, I'd have grown to become the person they told me I would be. And this, my dear Wais Na Misis, is how powerful your words can be.

It can be a joke or it can be something that's spoken out of an intense emotion—unintentional to say the least. But, words still hold the power to shape someone's life and reality, so choose to say the ones that are uplifting and encouraging. Your words can kill or bring something to life, always remember that.

WAIS TIP #60: BEAUTIFUL PEOPLE FORGIVE

I have received messages from random people and followers asking me how I was able to move on and forgive the people who have hurt me—the ones who have swindled my company, who have disrespected my home, who have spread rumours, and all the rest who have made me question why some people are just plainly mean. I have mentioned my healing process on my blog (which I haven't updated in years, by the way!) but I'll gladly share it, again, with you here:

1. I acknowledge that I was hurt. I don't deny what happened because if I do, I'd definitely become a ticking time bomb that can explode anytime I am triggered. So, instead of keeping it in, I allow myself to feel the pain, anger, or whatever it is that I need to feel at the moment. I give myself some time to feel the emotion and for my emotional wounds to heal.
2. If I still feel angry, instead of lashing out at people, I write it in my journal or on my blog. This helps me release all the negative emotions without hurting other people in the process. I let everything out, of course, with caution. I don't curse or belittle my oppressors just so I will feel better.
3. Once I get freed from my anger, I now make myself understand that I can never reverse the situation. No one has the power to do it, so it's best to just learn from it and slowly move forward. If I feel like I cannot forgive the person just yet, I go back to step 1. Otherwise, I will continue moving forward like a Wais and a mature person; taking with me the lessons I can use when the same thing happens again.
4. No matter how difficult it is at times, I always try to see the good in other people. I do my best to focus on the positive side of everyone and everything because life is short to dwell on the things that make us sad. Since I am the type of person who thrives in a happy and healthy environment, I make a conscious decision to live a life surrounded by good vibes. This isn't me promoting toxic

positivity or delusion, okay? I just truly believe that the world is still a beautiful place filled with beautiful people despite the bad things that have happened to me. Just be smart enough to cut off people or leave situations when it starts to negatively affect your physical, mental, and even spiritual health.

WAIS TIP #61: BEAUTIFUL PEOPLE KNOW THAT MONEY IS NOT THEIR ONLY TREASURE IN THIS WORLD

Because I know that money is a by-product of a lot of things and it can be taken away from me anytime, I invest in people, too. I give my time and energy to help hone their talents and their skills as much as I invest in tangible things like farms, resthouses, and beauty salons. I trust them with my businesses.

Speaking of beauty salons, this principle was one of the reasons why I chose to take over the salon business that was about to close down because of the pandemic. I didn't want it to close because I know that there are talented people behind the brand that will be left with no source of income once it happens.

WAIS TIP #62: BEAUTIFUL PEOPLE SERVE OTHERS

I work hard so I can serve my family well and give them a better life. I have written in my diary that I wanted to earn a lot when I was twenty-three years old because I wanted to give my parents a nice home. My dad had been working abroad and I wanted him and my mom to finally stop working because they were already getting old. Despite the emotional rollercoaster that they had given me, I still wanted to serve them for as long as I could.

I put up businesses and invest in properties so I can also put my God-given skills and opportunities so the people and the community around me can also benefit from them. Through the businesses that strive hard to manage, people from all walks are able to earn and make a living out of it. The gift that God has given me easily multiplies.

Chapter 20

Outer Beauty

If you are reading this chapter, congratulations, you have reached the last chapter of the book. But, if you have just skipped to this part, congratulations still. Now, go back to chapter one and start reading! Hehehe.

I have decided to end my highly emotional book with something light! You know, like a palate cleanser after a heavy meal. (See? I have learned something from my image and etiquette training after all!) Anyway, I have dedicated this final chapter to outer beauty, since we have just talked about inner beauty. Why? Because I believe that being a Wais Na Misis is also knowing how best to take care of your inner and most especially your outer self.

Being a little too busy is not a good reason to neglect yourself. You only have one YOU in this lifetime. You can't reorder another set if the first one breaks down. So, while you still have the time, start giving your body a bit more TLC. Because 1. It's the first thing that people will see and not your kind heart or witty humour; and 2. Looking good on the outside, no matter how superficial it may sound, can definitely make you feel good on the inside, too!

Don't know where to start? Allow me to share my personal beauty secrets and techniques so you have something to begin your beauty journey with. Have fun!

WAIS TIP #63: APPLY BODY OIL BEFORE SHOWERING

I don't usually apply lotion all over my body. Sometimes, I am too lazy to do it. So, instead, just before I take a shower, I apply virgin coconut oil on dry skin all over my body. As in all over. From my head to my armpits and down to the soles of my feet. Once done, I shower as usual. I always find my skin so soft, smooth, and highly moisturized after I do this. If you're not a fan of VCO, you can use any of your preferred body oils, too.

WAIS TIP #64: CREATE A SIMPLE SKINCARE ROUTINE

We are not getting any younger, my dear Wais Na Misis. With this reality comes the need to take good care of our skin more. This means it's time for you to have at least a simple skincare routine if you don't have one yet.

I have been asked many times to share my routine because, they said, they always notice how my skin would glow each time they see me on television or online. So, as a WAIS NA MISIS, we shouldn't just be goal-getters but we have to be 'glow-getters' as well.

Don't feel too pressured to buy the latest skincare set or follow the famous 10-Step Korean skincare routine. All you have to do is either consult with a dermatologist or do a thorough research to find your skin type. Once you have figured this one out, you can now ask your dermatologist for product recommendations, if you have special skin concerns, or you can head to the nearest department store to buy your basic skincare products.

It should include a cleanser, toner, moisturizer, serum (to target special skin concerns), and sunscreen for daytime use. With these products, you can already achieve healthy and glowing skin. Just remember to do the routine regularly and make sure that all the products work well together for the best results.

I also like massaging my face when I apply the moisturizer. If you have the extra time, please do it. Sometimes, I use the icy face massager to help relax my facial muscles.

Lastly, please do not forget to wear sunscreen. This is very important especially if you are the type to spend the day outdoors!

WAIS TIP #65: EAT YOUR GREENS!

You know what they say, you are what you eat. And this one remains true until today. Eating vegetables has a lot of health benefits which include improved outer appearance. Veggies are packed with vitamins, minerals, and antioxidants that help make our skin, hair, and nails look better and become stronger.

My fellow Wais Na Misis, this is what our backyard vegetable garden is for! Since our beauty secrets are just a garden away, we can easily incorporate these into our diet.

And in doing so, we will achieve better complexion and overall wellness.

If you're one to dislike chewing on veggies, you can at least try to juice it so you still get to have your daily vegetable fix. Or you can mix it with yummy sauces and eat it as a side salad. You can come up with as many tricks as you like to make sure that you don't skip on this abundant beauty ingredient.

WAIS TIP #66: DRINK LOTS OF WATER

This is a well-known fact, drinking water helps flush toxins out of our body which helps keep our skin looking clear and healthy. Doing this also helps to keep our skin hydrated which helps in reducing the appearance of fine lines and wrinkles. So, you better think twice before drinking that ice-cold soda.

As mentioned in the previous chapter, I drink a glass of warm water in the morning to jumpstart my digestive system. It also helps wake my body up and make me feel a bit full in the morning so I don't eat a lot. Sometimes, when I find my water too boring, I squeeze half a lemon to give it a little upgrade.

In addition to its skincare benefits, drinking enough water can also boost our overall health and well-being. It can help improve our digestion, and boost our energy levels and our immune system. All of which contributes to a healthier and more radiant appearance.

So, if you're looking for an additional step to add to your beauty routine, make sure to drink plenty of water throughout the day. Aim for at least eight glasses a day, and more if you're active or live in a hot climate. Your body and your skin will thank you!

WAIS TIP #67: WEAR SUNSCREEN

If you love the outdoors like me, you better not be skipping sunscreen! Because as we all know, constant exposure to UV rays from the sun can definitely lead to premature aging and sunburn, and it also increases your risk of skin cancer. Pretty scary right? But by applying sunscreen every day, you can somehow prevent these negative effects from happening. Just make sure to apply at least two fingers' worth of sunscreen on every part of your body and don't forget to re-apply after a few hours.

WAIS TIP #68: PUT ON MAKEUP AND FIX YOUR HAIR

One of the things I love about working in front of the camera is the part where I get the chance to have my hair and makeup done. Though tedious and sometimes unnecessary, looking good because of the way my hair and makeup is done creates a big impact on my self-confidence, at least for the day. I mean, it's a temporary fix, I know, but we all need this, especially on days when we need to look presentable and dignified.

You can always do it by yourself if you are trying to save money as having your hair and makeup professionally done can really cost you a lot. You can start by browsing through Youtube makeup tutorials by local and foreign beauty gurus alike. Actually, you won't have a hard time looking for one that suits your taste because the tutorials are everywhere. You just need to know where to look.

There are also beauty brands that offer free makeup services as part of their customer service program. Make the most out of it. But, if you have a little budget to spare you can go ahead and buy your starter set from the brand that you love. Don't be shy to share your budget with the salesperson. By doing this, you are actually helping them recommend a basic set for you that won't break your budget.

WAIS TIP #69: SLEEP FOR 8 HOURS OR MORE

When we were younger, we used to dislike sleeping because we would rather spend our days outside, playing than lie on the bed in the middle of the day. I would usually be forced to take afternoon naps as a child because I'd get a good spanking from my mom if I don't take it. Sleeping was a chore for me and I did it out of obedience. Now that I'm older, I take afternoon naps, not out of obedience any more but because my body now feels exhausted from all the day's work. If I don't take it, I'd overheat and I won't be able to function well.

Whenever you get a chance to sleep, please take it. Because you are also giving your body the chance to repair and regenerate so you can become healthier.

WAIS TIP #70: THINK HAPPY THOUGHTS!

Filling our heads with these kinds of thoughts can improve our appearance by somehow reducing our stress. As we all know, stress can really take a toll on our minds and bodies which will lead to more health issues and a tired-looking outer appearance. Plus, thinking happy thoughts helps our mindset to become better which makes us look more confident and attractive.

I am an advocate of happy thoughts. I love it because it keeps me young. Since I don't have any space for stressful stuff in my mind, I realize that I have become more creative and productive. It's as if my mind is well-calibrated for some reason.

Along with the happy thoughts is the conscious decision not to think of anything bad about other people. Yes, even when they do me wrong. Because, again, my mind is filled with lovely things, I don't have the headspace to wish anyone ill.

Epilogue

How are you, my fellow Wais Na Misis? I hope you had a great time reading through my thoughts and learning from my experience.

Allow me to thank you for supporting me from the start of my journey until today, the release of my very first book.

I pray that we get more opportunities to learn more from life and other WAIS NA MISIS so we can continue serving our families in the best possible way we can.

Thank you, again, for your unwavering support. I promise to keep on improving and innovating so I, together with other Wais Na Misis, can leave this world in a better state than I've found it.

And now that you are finished with this book, help others to become as Wais as you, too, by sharing it.

Until the next adventure!

Love,

Your Wais Na Misis
Neri Miranda

Acknowledgement

In the process of crafting this book, there are several remarkable individuals who I wish to express my deepest gratitude to. However, before I do so, I want to pay tribute to my number one teacher— God. It is through the kind of life He has allowed me to live and the experiences He has given me, that has shaped me into the person I am today. So, thank you, dear God!

To my incredible husband, Chito, you have been my mentor, confidante, and unwavering source of support in this lifetime. Your love has lifted me during both highs and lows, and your guidance has helped me navigate through the challenges of our lives. Your presence has provided the answers, the strength, and the comforting embrace I needed, to make it through this journey. I am forever grateful for the faith you have shown me.

To my extraordinary Mom who has taught me most of the 'Wais' ways I know, thank you. Your survival tips and tricks, and your solid determination to live a better life have greatly influenced me on how I would look at life. Growing up, you have taught me how to dream, how to embody strength, and how to persevere. From a young age, you have instilled in me the belief that no dream is too big. You encouraged me to reach for the stars, to break free from limitations, and to embrace the boundless possibilities that life has to offer. Thank you, Ma!

To my beloved children, Pia, Miggy, and Cash, you are all my inspiration, my driving force, and my greatest joy. Your presence in my life has given me a deep sense of purpose and has fueled my determination to create a brighter future for our family. Your innocent questions, unwavering faith, and unconditional love remind me daily of what truly matters in this life. I am forever grateful that I am your mom and I get to witness your own journeys unfold.

To my dearest supporters who have stood by me throughout this journey, I extend my heartfelt appreciation. Your encouragement, support, and belief in my abilities have been instrumental in my Wais Na Misis journey. Your being there has given me determination to do my best, because you all inspired me to never give up. Thank you.

To you who is holding this book and who is now with me on this adventure, thank you. I hope that my experiences shared within these pages will resonate with you. May they ignite your own dreams and empower you to live the best life you are meant to have. Thank you for choosing to read this book.